THE FINANCIAL PINWHEEL

BUILDING YOUR PERPETUAL FINANCIAL ENERGY MACHINE

THE FINANCIAL PINWHEEL[IP]

BUILDING YOUR PERPETUAL FINANCIAL ENERGY[IP] MACHINE

JOSEPH P. OKALY

ethos
collective

Printed in the United States of America

Published by Igniting Souls
PO Box 43, Powell, OH 43065
IgnitingSouls.com

LCCN: 2024920723
Paperback ISBN: 978-1-63680-392-0
Hardcover ISBN: 978-1-63680-393-7
e-book ISBN: 978-1-63680-394-4

Available in paperback, hardcover, e-book, and audiobook.

Any Internet addresses (websites, blogs, etc.) and telephone numbers printed in this book are offered as a resource. They are not intended in any way to be or imply an endorsement by Igniting Souls, nor does Igniting Souls vouch for the content of these sites and numbers for the life of this book.

Some names and identifying details may have been changed to protect the privacy of individuals.

The superscript symbol IP listed throughout this book is known as the unique certification mark created and owned by Instant IP™. Its use signifies that the corresponding expression (words, phrases, chart, graph, etc.) has been protected by Instant IP™ via smart contract. Instant IP™ is designed with the patented smart contract solution (US Patent: 11,928,748), which creates an immutable time-stamped first layer and fast layer identifying the moment in time an idea is filed on the blockchain. This solution can be used in defending intellectual property protection. Infringing upon the respective intellectual property, i.e., IP, is subject to and punishable in a court of law.

This book is dedicated to my children.
May you always have the courage to create
and share new ideas toward making
this world a better place.

Contents

Foreword

When you continually visit people in their homes for 30 years, you build a familial relationship. You know them better than you know most of your family members. In my early 60s, my wife, Savia, and I accepted the fact that we would eventually pass our financial planning business to someone else. Someone who was honest, knowledgeable, cared about our clients like we did, and could also run our growing business.

Where could we find such a person? Joe found us and in the most unexpected way! One of his mom's best friends had known him since he was two. She worked with us and saw Joe's mom regularly. Joe played with her kids growing up. When she heard that he was looking for an internship, she did not think to refer Joe. Her son and Joe grew up together and were longtime friends. They were actually roommates in college, sharing a hallway, shower, and refrigerator. Her son had even been an intern with us the previous summer, so he knew exactly what we did. He did not think of referring Joe either. The owner of one of the outside offices that I managed had Joe referred to her looking for an internship. She very well may have taken Joe on as an intern, but her son just so happened to be interning for her that year already. Instead, she finally referred Joe to us. That is how we met. Was it a coincidence that two people who worked with me and had known Joe since childhood, one of which who currently roomed with him, did not mention Joe, but a person he didn't even know sent him our way? I don't think so. **Fate would not be denied!**

After observing Joe as an intern, I offered him a job when he graduated, which he accepted. When he started, I asked him to learn all our concepts and systems. However, I also told him to ask questions, and if he thought something could be improved, to tell me, and we would discuss it. Well, we had many discussions. Before long, I had taught him everything from my 40 years of experience and knowledge, and he was then teaching me. That is how I knew this was the right person to continue what my wife and I had built.

At our firm, one of my responsibilities, as well as enjoyments, is teaching new employees and interns the game of chess. It is a wonderful mental exercise and contributes to our firm's core value of lifelong learning. I taught Joe chess. Just like with the business, before too long, he was teaching me here too. Why am I bringing this up? Financial Planning is not an easy career. You have to want to continually learn as everything keeps changing. You need to know about investments, insurance, mortgages, risk management, psychology, legal issues, taxes, and logic all in order to be able to design and present a plan to a client that they will understand. You have to make the complicated simple.

Past generations had a much simpler life. Most people had pensions and social security. Bank interest rates were 5% or higher, and retirement age and life expectancy were close together. Investments seemed exotic, risky, and unnecessary. Times have changed. With a dramatic increase in life expectancy and fewer pensions, social security and bank interest are no longer capable of providing retirement income. Investments are now needed to supplement our income. However, the education and knowledge regarding finances are still not taught in school.

Hundreds of individuals and families, whom we regard as our extended family, depend on us for advice. Our goal, from the beginning, was helping people with their finances so their lives could be more enjoyable. We came to a point where we realized that we were not really making a dent in spreading financial education. We needed a new strategy.

I began writing a book on financial planning based on my 40 years of experience, but when Joe gave me his Financial Pinwheel book to read, I realized my book was not needed. The book you are holding in your hand is the new strategy. It is designed to bring our knowledge and experience to more people and spread the word that you don't have to be worried about money. By reading Joe's book, you will be joining our extended family and learning the concepts we have taught hundreds of clients. You will gain perspective on how all these seemingly random financial pieces fit together. His analogy using a pinwheel is genius. He is organized, logical, and entertaining not only in his book but also in real life. While we have taught each other much in our lives, one common core belief was a desire to help as many people as we could. This was always our shared dream.

Welcome to our family. Enjoy your journey!

Robert Giarraffa

Introduction

A Pinwheel in Perpetual Motion[IP]

A young girl in a summer dress skips across her yard. Her bare feet feel the coolness of the grass as her flower dress dances in rhythm with her movements. Freeness radiates from her being. You need not ask her if she feels joy.

She comes upon a pinwheel in the yard, four blades tucked neatly together in unison. Blowing into the pinwheel, there are huge expectations, though, to her surprise, it spins very little. She is but a child. Again and again, she tries, with each succession employing the most giant breaths she can muster. The pinwheel moves only slightly more, though, quickly coming back to rest. As her frustration mounts, her joy subsides.

Running to her father, she asks him to make the pinwheel spin. He takes a deep breath and sends the pinwheel spinning, her face lighting up as the blades go round. This time, too, it starts to slow, though not as immediately as with her attempts.

"Why does it stop?" she asks.

"Well, it needs more wind, more energy," her father replies. He holds it high above his head to catch the summer breeze rising behind them.

Again, the girl's face lights up, and it spins longer than any time before.

"That's it, that's it!" she shouts.

After a minute, though, the wind subsides, the blades slow, and once again, the pinwheel comes to rest.

Looking at the pinwheel and then inquisitively at her father, she asks, "Daddy, how can we make it spin forever?"

This is the conversation I had with my daughter, which inspired the premise of this book. How to make the pinwheel spin forever. A pinwheel in perpetual motion. While in the physical world, a perpetual motion machine is impossible, in the financial world, it is a premise that can be achieved.

The pinwheel is what you may initially think of as your expenses, what you need to live your life in the way you choose. The pinwheel is your desired lifestyle. The pinwheel spinning is these needs being met, the lifestyle you desire being accomplished. As long as the pinwheel keeps spinning, you are meeting your lifestyle needs.

When we are young, we have no way of powering our pinwheel. It may be smaller, but we have nothing to make it move, no financial energy to power it. Our parents provide the financial energy. They buy our diapers, baby food, clothes, sports equipment, dance lessons, iPads, cell phones—everything we need. As we get older, this eventually changes. We obtain jobs. We now need to power our pinwheel on our own for the rest of our lives. We just were never taught how to do this effectively.

The Financial Pinwheel is broken into four parts, just like the four blades of most common pinwheels. While the concepts are universal, there are varying contexts based on how you create your own financial energy. For example, you may work in a government job with a pension or a Fortune 500 company that has a 401(k), or you may be an entrepreneur owning your own company. Each of these requires a different set of rules to generate the perpetual financial energy you need for your pinwheel. There is no right or wrong; there is simply a different game we are choosing to play, a different set of rules that are true for building our perpetual pinwheel.

If you look at the most notable financial books, there are a number of similarities. For one, most do not differentiate the ways of creating financial energy. If they do discuss them, in my opinion, they generally are advocating one method, almost universally entrepreneurial approaches, while often showing contempt for the alternatives. This is likely because most of the authors are entrepreneurs themselves, with surprisingly few of the most successful having backgrounds in financial planning or advising. Each of us has a different skill set and comfort level, though—entrepreneurship isn't for everyone. So, while we should certainly be made aware of the rules we are signing up to play by when we step into one of these arenas of employment, each can successfully produce the financial energy needed for a perpetual pinwheel.

The second similarity is most financial books do not provide overly specific advice. As human beings, we relate more to stories than formulas, so I leave it to you to explore this book in as much depth as you would like. The general concept of the pinwheel, and each subsequent section, can be viewed as a high-level shift in perspective, or you can utilize the additional resources and tools I've created both in this book and at TheFinancialPinwheel.com to take on more specific elements and planning.

If you leave the book with a better understanding of where you are, how your lifestyle relates to your financial energy created, and how to get closer to having that financial energy power a perpetual pinwheel, then my goal for you will be achieved.

The Fables We're Told

You have probably heard the story of "The Ants and the Grasshopper," one of Aesop's Fables. It goes something like this.

> In late autumn, some ants were drying out the grain they had worked all summer to collect. A starving grasshopper, fiddle under his arm, comes up and begs for a bite to eat. The ants exclaim their shock that the grasshopper hasn't stored any food. When he explains he was too busy making music all summer, losing track of the time, they laugh and mock him, telling him to dance for a bite to eat.

Aesop was trying to illustrate the importance of hard work. He, however, left out the rest of the story. There was... wait for it...another grasshopper! The rest of the story goes something like this.

> Before long, another grasshopper came along. The ants immediately mocked him, assuming he, too, was coming to beg for a bite to eat. He politely corrected them, as he had more than enough food to last the entire winter. Every morning, he had collected just a few grains and stored them away, leaving the rest of the day to make music. How sad the ants' summer must have been if all they did was work. Perhaps they would like to hear a tune to give them some joy?

The full version of this fable, well, at least my full version, illustrates that there is much more of a balance than we are led to believe. While the first grasshopper is obviously not a model to emulate, ignoring his future needs altogether, the ants are perhaps not one to follow. Sure, if you had to pick, the ant model is safer, but blindly storing as much food as possible leaves you exhausted and with missed opportunities for joy.

Do you know how long the average garden ant worker lives? Just 1–2 years. The queen ant, who does not collect any grain at all, mind you, lives up to 28 years. Clearly, the worker ant's life is not what we want for ourselves.

The second grasshopper understood his needs and was, therefore, able to establish a plan to meet them. His pinwheel needed so many pieces of grain to be powered through the winter. So, he stored a few each morning, putting them away for himself first, and by the end of the summer, he had more than enough stored. Because he wasn't blindly storing as much as possible but rather had clarity on the amount he needed, he was free of anxiety with the confidence to spend the rest of his day enjoying the sun and making music. We, too, should be free to experience joy.

We can make decisions in one of two ways. The first is making a decision based on what we have already learned up to this point in time. The second is by learning something new.

If you are reading this, you must be open to the second way. And because the financial education provided to us in school is so poor, more accurately, nonexistent, what you already have learned up to this point in time may very well be limited to passing comments from friends and family. Discussions on finances tend to be considered taboo, even with your closest relatives. It is inappropriate to ask others about money.

Most Americans feel this way. If you have anxiety, uneasiness, or a sense of intimidation when it comes to finances, then you are pretty much like everyone else. You may think your friends and family have it figured out. They don't. You may see people wearing designer clothes, driving fancy cars, and living in big houses and assume they must have wealth. They likely do not.

We cannot be proficient, nevermind excel, in something we were never taught. Shakespeare and chemistry are all well and good, but neither will help you with something every employed adult has to manage—their finances.

I grew up in Denville, NJ. It is a stop on a commuter train line to New York City. I always assumed that New York City was where I would work. I went to The College of New Jersey, majoring in Finance, and it wasn't until a random guest speaker came to class that my vision changed. This speaker called himself a Financial Planner, which I had never heard of before, but when I learned that I could work with math and numbers (sorry, math nerd, it is really super fun) and help normal, middle-class people achieve their goals, all while not commuting into the city, I was like…sign me up!

I wound up interning at a firm, New Horizons Wealth Management, which specializes in assisting middle and upper-middle-class families, and was offered a full-time position after I graduated. I learned directly from the firm's founder about cash flow, investments, insurance, and comprehensive financial planning. He also modeled a very important lesson: Having every aspect of your situation be mutually supportive enables you to accomplish your goals in life. Naturally, I used these teachings for my own situation and started to secure a strong financial foundation for myself at age 22. I had unknowingly been given a supreme gift— financial literacy—that no one around me seemed to have.

When hanging out with friends or family, I realized that no one seemed to have much of an idea of what was going on with their finances. I would hear people joke about working until they were 100 years old or picking only their favorite child to attend college due to the expense. They viewed finances not as a source of opportunity but rather as a source of anxiety as they sailed through the fog of a complicated unknown. Something needed to shift, and I realized it was an opportunity I could step into.

Now, over 15 years later, I own the firm where I once interned. I have helped hundreds of families reach their goals and retire. You go through retirement once in your life. I go through it weekly. I have seen people cry in my office when a financial burden was lifted off them as the unknown fog was cast aside with the relief of clarity. I have seen expressions of disbelief when finding out more money must actually be spent in retirement. I look forward to annual reviews so I can hear the additional joy created through my encouragement to take that extra trip to Disney World or put in a pool for the family. I love my job. Actually, scratch that. I love my *purpose*.

This book is an extension of my purpose, to help in giving as many people these same feelings. I can't personally work with everyone, so I've designed a system—The Financial Pinwheel—to provide you with the financial education absent from your school years, along with a process you can enact to gain clarity and control. The process comes with tools, both in this book and through additional resources at TheFinancialPinwheel.com. Great possibilities await you.

The Long Line of the Pinwheel

My favorite version of the national anthem is performed by John Brancy, a Grammy-winning Baritone, who shares his talents before select New York Rangers hockey games. Anticipation builds as I see him walk out of the tunnel, a clean-shaven head with a tightly trimmed beard, donning a well-fitted tux and a Rangers scarf around his neck. He looks energized, his face on the cusp of breaking out into a full smile for what he is about to share. Excitement fills me like getting into the car of a thrill ride, as I know he will pull me through the course of the performance. You don't hear him; you feel him take you through the passage, his deep, mesmerizing tone leaving you with goosebumps by the end.

The words that John sings are no different than those of any other performer, though. Every national anthem performer is more or less consistent with the general tone. The totality of the performance and the feeling you are left with—the long line—is the difference. The long line of the music is how a performance feels as it takes you through the piece. If you broke it into tiny sections—short lines—every performer would be the same, and you would lose the depth and feeling that the long line delivers.

Here's another example. Alternatively when we scroll through social media, we are bombarded with short lines of information—quick tips and headlines: Top 5 credit cards for rewards. The 10 best trips on a budget. The top 3 car lease deals this month. Short lines of information. The long line is lost. These short bits of information are minimally helpful on their own and, without a long line to tie them together, become lost and ineffective. I don't want to provide you with a grab bag of financial techniques. I want to provide you with a new way of looking at the structure of your financial choices. I want to give you a long line you can follow.

This isn't just to help you. It helps everyone around you. If you feel more confident, not richer, mind you, but more confident financially, then you will have less to fear. If you feel confident that the next step you are taking is solid, then you will have less anxiety and more opportunities for happiness. Your happiness affects your spouse, your children, your neighbor, your coworkers. Understanding what you can do allows you to give more to your family, parents, and great causes.

Following the long line doesn't even have to mean you give your money. If you have freedom of money, then you have the power to create freedom of time. If you have freedom of time, you have the means for freedom of purpose. The goal doesn't have to be a higher position because more money for the sake of more money is walking blindly in the dark of our true needs. If we turn the light on, we can choose to be at more soccer games and breakfasts with parents. More service in our community. This is to benefit everyone around you.

As such, before we jump into the various parts that comprise it, let's first look at the long line of the Financial Pinwheel. To start, I want you to visualize a pinwheel in your mind. You blow into the pinwheel, spinning it round and round. Now, picture the pinwheel increasing in size. These are your expenses; your lifestyle is getting bigger. Feel how it is harder to spin.

Now, picture a stronger wind coming, the breeze picking up. This is your income increasing. It is strong enough to power this pinwheel. So much so that there is energy left over. You capture some of this extra financial energy. It is redirected into a battery, stored energy for you later. The battery starts off small, but you can picture it slowly getting bigger and bigger the more energy you place into it. The more energy you save, the bigger your financial battery gets.

Attached to the battery is a solar panel. As the sun's energy beats down on the dark panel, you can see energy now flowing into your battery. Your battery is now not only being powered by you but is growing all by itself, compounding its size and growth. You can see the battery growing even more quickly than before.

Finally, it is so large that you stop blowing your pinwheel altogether. You switch on your financial battery. Your pinwheel keeps spinning. You are doing nothing. The battery is powering the pinwheel completely without you. The energy lost from powering your pinwheel is replenished back into the battery by the attached solar panel. Your pinwheel is now perpetual. It is spinning on its own, forever for you.

Four Parts of the Financial Pinwheel

As we lean into the long line of the financial pinwheel throughout this book, you will feel your financial confidence grow as you learn to harness the financial energy you already create to build a pinwheel that can spin perpetually for you.

Here are the four parts of the financial pinwheel the long line will deliver:

1. Creating a Breeze (Pinwheel Size, Lifestyle Expenses, and Employment Arena)
2. Managing the Flow (Financial Energy Saved, Financial Batteries, and Account Types)
3. A Self-Charging Wind Machine (Charging the Batteries with Investments)
4. Preparing for the Hurricane (Protecting Your Pinwheel with Insurance)

All of these contain one or more tools here in the book, as well as extended self-guided options at TheFinancial-Pinwheel.com.

PART 1

Creating a Breeze

It Starts with a Breeze

My first material job was waiting tables at the Rattlesnake Ranch Cafe in high school. I would walk away with $150 or more on some nights. I felt infinitely rich.

This was because all my needs were already being met—I had no responsibility to pay for rent or internet or anything else living at home. This was all just discretionary income to spend. If I were to break this out as a full-time arrangement, it would look much different, though: $150/day for five days per week is just around $40,000 per year. Not exactly considered a substantial sum.

When you first start working after high school or college, your expenses tend to be minimal. Your pinwheel is very small, so even if you have modest financial energy in the form of an entry-level salary, you can power your pinwheel without much effort. Many young adults live at home for a time after finishing school to save money, an excess of financial energy due to such a small pinwheel. Recently, it has become more of a necessity for some, with excessive college debts causing a much larger and unsustainable financial pinwheel from a very early age. A $200,000 college debt could require repayment of over $2,300/mo, amounting to almost 70% of an entry-level $40,000 salary just to pay the loan.

Your financial energy isn't that strong starting out; it is a breeze, with income closely matching expenses. Your pinwheel turns, but if you stopped working tomorrow, your pinwheel would immediately stop. No financial energy has been stored, and no financial batteries exist. A positive cash flow allows you to do the things you want in life today, but it is not enough beyond that.

When people see large pinwheels spinning—big houses, fancy cars, lavish vacations—they relate this with wealth. Spinning a large pinwheel temporarily and spinning a large pinwheel forever are two very different things, however. Wealth is what you have built up, not what you spend.

Consider professional athletes. A 2009 Sports Illustrated report estimated that 78% of National Football League

(NFL) players file for bankruptcy or are experiencing financial stress only two years after retiring, and 60% of National Basketball Association (NBA) players suffer the same fate after five years of retirement.[1] Former heavyweight boxing champion Mike Tyson, once worth a reported 400M, declared bankruptcy in 2003 prior to even retiring.[2] Olympic and World Championship figure skater Dorothy Hamill turned pro soon after her 1976 gold medal win.

Despite the millions earned skating in professional shows like the Ice Capades, by 1996, she had declared bankruptcy.[3] Allen Iverson, an NBA star most notably known for playing with the Philadelphia 76ers, earned over $150 million, not counting his sponsorship deals.[4] When I was in middle school, I wore Allen Iverson basketball shoes, and yes, if you were wondering, they made me notably better. By 2012, he couldn't pay his debts, reportedly spending $10,000/mo on clothing alone.

Spinning a large pinwheel temporarily may require a substantial income—a strong wind of financial energy. If the income stops, though, the large pinwheel stops too. Spinning a large pinwheel forever takes something very different. It takes wealth. Wealth is having a self-charging financial battery. A financial battery to power your pinwheel forever after the wind from your job stops completely.

The subsequent sections of this book will teach you how to create the wealth you need—this self-charging financial battery—but first, you need to determine how big of a pinwheel you want to spin.

The Size of Your Pinwheel

I had a client who was a doctor. He shared that when he made $100,000, he couldn't save anything. When he made

$200,000, he somehow couldn't save anything. Finally, he made $500,000, and he still couldn't save enough. You may look at these numbers and, based on your own situation, quite possibly be judgmental of this individual. If you look at your own income, though, over the last five years, how much of your income growth have you saved?

Universally, incomes go up over time. If they didn't, we would have no way of paying for ever-increasing expenses. We meet with our clients annually, so we are in a position to see these changes. Our rough estimate from reviewing our client data is around 5% long-term. Wage data from 1960 to 2024 showed an average even higher at 6.19%.

At our lower 5%, a $100,000 income turns into around $127,500 in five years. Income has increased by 27.5%. There are only two options for this increase, as it can't disappear. Either it is spent (bigger pinwheel), or it is saved (bigger financial batteries).

Financial Energy Flow Tradeoff[fp]

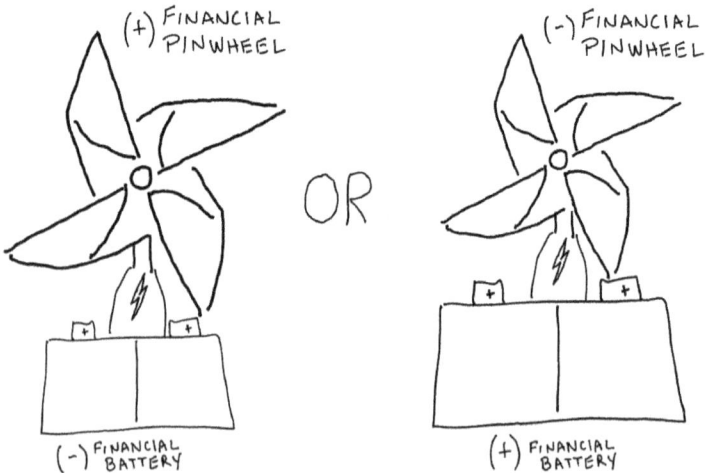

If you were to look at your tax return from five years ago, how much has your income changed? How much more financial energy is now being produced, and more importantly, has it all just gone into a bigger pinwheel?

Most people have the size of their pinwheels dictated to them instead of being intentional in its creation. We make more money. We spend more money. When we spend more, we become accustomed to more. Our pinwheel grows without us even knowing. Consider the alternative. We make more money. *We save more money.* We are no longer defaulting to more income, resulting in an equally larger pinwheel.

We get to determine the size of our pinwheel through greater intentionality and awareness. First though, we need to see where we are starting today.

Measuring Your Pinwheel Today

When most people try to budget, they attempt to account for every penny of their expenses. It is tedious, time-consuming, and really unenjoyable. You spend hours organizing, and then the dog gets sick and blows the whole thing up. Most people don't last more than a few months trying this method.

While this method logically makes sense in trying to see where everything is going, we need to find solutions that we can actually implement and sustain. Instead of trying to figure out where everything is going, we are going to just put everything into two buckets: Savings and Expenses.

Savings is listed first intentionally. The focus is first on what you are saving, paying yourself first. If you pay yourself enough first, and let's face it, you are worth it, then where the rest of your money is going doesn't really matter. You don't need to know if it is going more to Starbucks, the driving range, or the nail salon. No two pinwheels are the same.

This method makes calculating your pinwheel a very simple exercise. It shifts the focus to something positive—saving towards yourself, building those financial batteries—instead of trying in vain to itemize an ever-changing list of expenses.

To perform this exercise, start with your take-home pay, which is the amount you receive after all taxes and deductions. Only focus on your actual take-home income for the calculation. If you save $500/mo into your work plan, 401(k) or otherwise, that comes out *before* you receive your take-home pay, so it should not be included. To keep the math simple, let's say your total household take-home pay is $10,000/mo.

If you don't save anything from your take-home pay, then you already know the size of your pinwheel. It is $10,000/mo. If you, for example, saved $1,000/mo into your investment account, 10% of your take-home income, then you would know the size of your pinwheel is $9,000/mo.

Additionally, something only qualifies as savings if you never spend it, not if you just temporarily put it aside. For example, if you put $100/mo into a savings account but then use the money once per year on a vacation, it is not really being saved. It is being spent—just later. A good way to tell if it is really being saved is to look at the accounts over time. The account should be increasing. If you save $100/mo, then in six months, the account should be $600 higher. In a year, it should be $1,200 higher. In two years, $2,400 higher. Look at your account six months ago. Is it growing by the amount you feel you are saving?

For purposes right now, though, measure your own financial pinwheel. How big is it? This is one of the digital tools that can be found at TheFinancialPinwheel.com.

Measuring Your Financial Pinwheel[IP]

My household take-home pay is:
_____ (ex: 10,000/mo)

My savings from my take-home pay are:
_____ (ex: 1,000/mo)

The size of my Financial Pinwheel is:
_____ (ex: 10,000-1,000 = 9,000/mo)

Note: For those who may have more variable income, whether through larger commissions, business flows, or otherwise, it may be easier to measure annually. So, for example, $120,000/yr take-home pay, with $12,000/yr saved from that take-home pay, will result in a $108,000/yr-sized pinwheel.

How long did that take? 30 seconds? Are you surprised by the size of your pinwheel?

We will incorporate all savings, including work savings, as well as how much you should be saving overall in the subsequent chapters.

Pinwheel Debt and 36%[IP]

You may be wondering how credit cards play into measuring your pinwheel. As long as you pay off your credit cards every month, you don't have to worry about them. It flows temporarily through the card and then is paid off with your earnings. I do this myself, funneling as much as I can through my card *for expenses I would have spent anyway* and receiving card benefits as a result. I personally prefer hotel or travel cards as those force me to take time and enjoy life with the benefits versus cash back that likely would just disappear.

If you do not pay off your credit card at the end of the month, then that is a different story. This is you making your pinwheel bigger than your financial energy can support. Why is credit card debt so hard to pay off? Well, if you didn't have enough financial energy at the start, which required the credit card in the first place, why would you have enough financial energy to pay it off now?

This doesn't mean all debt is bad. Some kinds of debt are inevitable, like a mortgage or a car, as you likely cannot save up the full price of the funds in advance. A mortgage, for example, is considered good debt.

However, your financial energy being created still needs to be able to support the payments for those items. Many times, a large house or an expensive car are the reasons that too little is left over for the rest of life's expenses. In these cases where credit cards are not able to be paid off at the end of the month, they may grow at 20% or more in interest, making an unsupportable pinwheel even less stable over time. Avoiding credit card debt here is the best approach. If you find yourself unable to only use the credit card for expenses that you would take on anyway, therefore having an inability to pay it off at the end of the month, then not having credit cards at all would likely be best. If this is you, don't worry; you are not alone. Credit card companies pay out a lot in perks and offer 0% incentives, yet still make a lot of money. This is because they know how many people struggle with managing this aspect.

When it comes to determining how much to take on with some of these larger expenses, a good ratio to try and stick to is not spending more than 36% of your gross (pre-tax) income on these generally fixed living expenses. If it seems oddly specific, it is because the mortgage industry created it. If you go to apply for a mortgage, they know that roughly 36% can be used on specific to you, often fixed, expenses. These would be items such as the mortgage, rent, auto loan/lease, and student loans—liabilities that some people may have and other people may not have. The other 64% they just ignore, as these go to items such as taxes, groceries, and internet—expenses common to everyone. For clients, we use an exercise called Backdoor Budgeting^{TM}, which leverages these ratios to help calculate savings ability.

As an example, if someone is earning $10,000/mo gross (pre-tax), we know that $3,600 can be used for the expenses specific to them. Their mortgage, car payments, and even something like daycare should all add up to less than 36%. This bucket is also where the savings come from, though, so if you are spending up to the 36% just on these specific to you expenses, then you likely do not have any additional room to save.

Finishing the example above, if your mortgage and car payments were the only fitting expenses here and came out to $2,600/mo, then you should have roughly an additional $1,000/mo to save toward yourself.

This exercise can be a bit trickier to run through, as it may be hard to determine what may fall into each bucket at times, so I mention it more as a guideline tool you can utilize if helpful. Even here, though, remember the goal is not to calculate a really specific number for expenses; the goal is to help you quickly get to a number you can commit towards saving.

The Path to Mulberry Street

One of the most impactful lessons I learned in school was from my finance professor, Dr. Mayo. It was not a lesson involving formulas or equations or anything financial in nature, for that matter, but rather a simple story that has stayed with me.

Dr. Mayo was of shorter stature, older in years but still with a thick head of gray hair combed over above his academic spectacles. In cartoon form, he would be Carl Fredrickson from the Pixar movie *Up*. If he had moved at a slower, more deliberate pace, it would have perfectly fit my expectations. To the contrary, though, he had enormous energy, engaging the class and drawing out discussions to support the underlying financial concepts we were to master.

In one such session, he asked the class how we would get to Mulberry Street, one of the roads a little bit off from the main campus. He called on people randomly in the class, each providing a different answer. As it turns out, there were many ways to get to Mulberry Street.

There are many ways to create the breeze, too—the financial energy to power your Financial Pinwheel. We need to be made more aware of what these options are and, more importantly, the tradeoffs that are involved in taking one route over another.

I was a finance major because my father was a Vice President of a large roofing company. He was in business, and I just so happened to choose business. My wife, Lauren, went to school for teaching. Her mother, as it just so happened again, was a teacher. While not always the case, of course, we often follow in our parents' footsteps. Why is that?

I believe it is because we are often asked the question of what we would like to be at an age where we are not mature enough to answer. We have also not been exposed sufficiently to all the possible paths. If my father was a mechanic, an attorney, or owned a landscaping company, that likely would have had an effect on what I saw as being possible through the lens of familiarity.

I have a client, Jennifer, who shared with me just how deliberate she was with her daughter growing up. In Jennifer's childhood, her father was often overlooked for positions he was otherwise qualified for due to his lack of a college degree. College education was, therefore, a focus for her and her siblings, but she found that it went even further than that. Her brother graduated with a college degree but had to work as a waiter for some time after college before landing a career in his field. It created greater intentionality for Jennifer, not only in going to college but also in how that degree translated to finding real work.

So, when Jennifer became a parent, she not only asked her daughter what she might like to do, but she also asked her what lifestyle she wanted to live. I love this second question. She asked her daughter lifestyle questions, such as how big of a house she saw herself living in and what kind of car she saw herself driving. If that is the lifestyle she wanted, the pinwheel she saw herself creating, then that should be considered prior to deciding on her career. The financial energy she was to create would have to power the pinwheel she imagined.

When you go to school, the degree is the asset you are purchasing. Looking at the return on investment, then, only makes sense. For example, when buying a house, the bank will not loan you more than the house is worth. Earlier, we spoke about how a $200,000 college loan could require a payment of over $2,300/mo. Think about what return on investment—what financial energy potential from that career—is required to make it a worthwhile venture. Even if your parents may be paying for all or a part of it, would you not want the return to be positive? If your desired pinwheel is $5,000/mo, well, now this college degree, this asset, better be able to return to you $7,300/mo ($5,000 pinwheel + $2,300 loan), or you will not have enough for the pinwheel you desire.

I'm not advocating that money buys happiness. Quite the contrary, as your desired lifestyle could be a tiny house in the middle of the country, a pinwheel that is quite a bit easier to support. At the same time, it should have an intentionality, as there are lifestyle elements we all picture having. I'm not ashamed to say I wanted a home large enough for each of my children to have their own bedroom and a yard they could play in. These play a part in how large my pinwheel is and, subsequently, how much financial energy my job needs to create in order to spin it consistently.

Focusing solely on what every school guidance counselor seems to ask, what would you enjoy doing, we rob the individual of consideration for the second part of the equation: what lifestyle you want to live. Mark Twain's old adage, "Find a job you enjoy doing, and you will never have to work a day in your life," is quite poetic but lacks real-life practicality. It can be too much like the first grasshopper, happy but hungry.

We want to intentionally select the path we take to Mulberry Street by first knowing what each path entails. If we are starting out in our lives, we can be more intentional from the start. However, for most, we may already be working in a certain area, and therefore, the goal becomes to better understand our current employment arena and how we can use it to attain that perpetual pinwheel.

Arenas of Employment[IP]

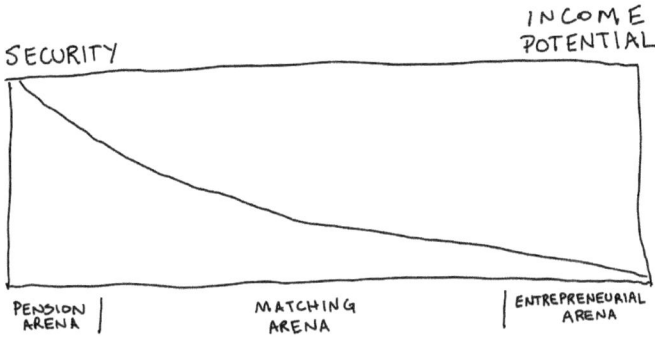

Now that you have measured your Financial Pinwheel and answered the question, "What lifestyle do I want to live," you should probably know how to have your specific employment arena build your perpetual pinwheel. I have organized all jobs into three main employment arenas. While these descriptions may not fit every job variation out there, they encompass the vast majority that we are familiar with. If you have a job now, you are currently in one of these three employment arenas. You may have chosen your arena intentionally, or like many people, you may have wound up in your arena by happenstance. They all create the financial energy you need to power your pinwheel, but each has its own benefits and drawbacks if you choose them as the path you take.

The Pension Arena[IP]

The first of two time-for-money arenas is the Pension Arena. You provide your time, and in exchange for your time, you receive a paycheck. It is also the arena that virtually the entire older generation participated in. They went to work every day, had enough to live on plus a little bit of discretionary spending, and retired with a corporate pension (employer) and government pension (social security) to get them through their later years. Their take-home income almost always equaled the size of their Financial Pinwheel. Most of them depended very little on additional investment income or savings for retirement, as pension incomes were enough. The great depression mindset had shaped them to pay off their mortgage, be careful in spending their money, and live on what they had. They were excellent at making sure their pinwheel was not larger than their financial energy. When the financial energy from working subsided, they had their financial batteries charged sufficiently through pensions to power their pinwheel for the rest of their life.

In today's world, corporate pensions are largely a thing of the past, with most remaining pensions residing in government work and unionized labor. A teacher is a prime example of this, often receiving a pension from the state (local pension) in addition to a federal government pension (social security). The tradeoff in the current pension arena is employment security for income potential. You probably have not heard yourself saying, "Wow, look at that Rollys-Royce, they must be a teacher!" or "Woah, look at that mansion by the ocean. I bet we see a US postal employee walk out!"

This is not in any way to marginalize the value of teachers, postal employees, or any unionized or government workers. They all play a hugely important role in their contributions to our society. I am not telling them anything they do not know when I say their income is more limited than those operating in the other employment arenas. A 2024 New York Federal Reserve analysis found that elementary and early childhood education were among the lowest salaries right after college and stayed that way mid-career—those aged 35 to 45—while being joined by other areas such as general education, secondary education, and social services.[5]

In the Pension Arena, you receive job security and a pension. These are your advantages if you choose to operate here. The main tradeoff given up in this arena is income potential. You will almost certainly not receive as high of an income, and so your Financial Pinwheel will have to be sized accordingly to manage the financial energy you are able to create. This last point, ironically enough, becomes one of your biggest advantages as well.

Let's look at an example. Timothy Teacher is 62 and retiring. He calculated his Financial Pinwheel (take-home pay minus take-home pay savings) to be $60,000/yr.

He has $70,000/yr in total pension income, with $20,000 via social security (government pension) and $50,000 via his pension from the state for teaching (local pension). His financial batteries, solely consisting of pensions in this example, likely cover the vast majority, if not all, of his expense needs. He has created a perpetual pinwheel.

While Timothy did not have as much discretionary income during his working years, it kept his lifestyle—his financial pinwheel—to a modest size, which made it easier to power in retirement. He also received a pension from the state that most do not receive. In many ways, this arena makes retirement the easiest. There are no shortcuts, the lifestyle will be more modest, and you have to put in your time, but it is hard not to stay on track.

Without the pension from the state, he would have had a sizable gap. The other two subsequent employment arenas need to fill this gap on their own. This is part of the reason why they need more income. They require more self-savings to power their financial battery for retirement. This comes in the form of retirement investments. I will discuss this more in the next sections.

If you convert the local pension into a retirement investment equivalent, it is a surprisingly large number to most. The rule of thumb for retirement investments is a 4% withdrawal. Essentially, this is how much you can withdraw and not run out of money.[6] So, if you divide what you receive from the pension by this number, in this example, $50,000 / 4%, you get to $1,250,000. Over 1 million dollars. It may not feel the same as actually having a million dollars in your investment account, but it is essentially an equivalent nonetheless. This is what the other two employment arenas would need to save up to replace an equivalent lifestyle.

The other pension source, social security, is influenced by earnings, but there is a cap, so it will not proportionally cover higher-earning individuals. In this example, social security accounts for around 30% of income needs ($20,000 / $60,000). For someone earning $250,000, they might receive $35,000/yr at the same age—almost double Timothy—but it would only account for 15% of their income needs as they probably have become accustomed to a much larger pinwheel at that level of earnings for so long.

Pension Arena Overview

Description: Those jobs receive a pension and job security as their primary benefits. Examples include teachers, postal employees, and other government workers.

Advantages

- Pension provides future guaranteed income
- Social security provides higher % coverage of future needs
- Modest income limits lifestyle expenses = Manageable Pinwheel
- Hard not to stay on track if you put in the time

Disadvantages

- Income opportunity is likely much more limited
- Discretionary spending will need to be less
- May not support the size of the desired Financial Pinwheel

Best Fit Statement: I want a job with a high degree of security where I am not required to save much to retire. I am willing to live a modest lifestyle with more limited discretionary spending, or I have a spouse in a different arena that may provide my discretionary spending flexibility.

The Matching Arena[IP]

The second of the two time-for-money arenas was previously part of the Pension Arena. The Matching Arena is where the vast majority of people reside. Everything from cashier to CEO falls into this arena.

The first private pension was created by American Express in 1875.[7] The life expectancy at that time was 39.4 years—significantly less than today, for sure.[8] As people began living longer and longer, pensions needed to be paid out for extended periods of time. They became burdensome for companies, which is why they have now largely been phased out.

Instead of providing a pension, which a company needs to manage, plan, and promise to pay out indefinitely, they switched to what are called defined contribution plans. They will give you extra money in the form of retirement contributions, but it will be up to you to manage, plan for sufficiency, and ultimately distribute.

As the retirement and savings burden is passed much more onto you, a larger income is generally also possible. With great power (income) comes great responsibility (savings).

There is such a wide range of possibilities in this arena, but the stereotypical story goes something like this. You take an entry-level position. You are not making that much money, just enough to power your small pinwheel. You get a promotion, though, and your income jumps up. You get a job offer from another company, and your income jumps up again. You may have started at $4,000/mo take-home pay, but now you may be at $8,000/mo. These increases provide both opportunity and potential hazards.

Your financial pinwheel probably became larger along the way in this story. You may have bought a house. You may have purchased a nicer car. It is natural to focus more on building the pinwheel you want than charging the batteries, which will need to power it later. In this arena, though, it is on you to save, which is drastically different from the Pension Arena, where they save for you. They may take out 10% of your pay automatically from day one and put it toward your future pension funding. There is no choice. This is where the potential hazards come into play. If you wait too long to start saving—to start creating those financial batteries—then you may find yourself unable to stop working. You'll need to continuously create your own financial energy for the large pinwheel you have become accustomed to spinning.

However, there is also a great opportunity present. You can choose to direct some of these increases in financial energy to your financial batteries instead. You get to choose where it is invested, giving you much greater control in creating your wealth.

I mentioned how, in the Pension Arena, they may automatically take 10% of your income toward your pension funding. Let's say you take that same 10% in our example to save. The $8,000/mo income would mean $800/mo saved. We will subsequently cover where this can go and how it can be invested, but for now, we will say it is earning 7% long-term. In 15 years, this would be calculated to be over $250,000. In 30 years, as the money grows on itself, it would calculate to be just shy of $1M.

Not too shabby, but we're still not quite where we need to be compared to the pension example (1.25M). There are two additional pieces here we still need to add in, though.

The first is that your contributions should increase over time as your income grows if you maintain that 10% savings rate. For example, if you get a promotion and make $9,000, now $900 is 10%. By saving more as your income grows (5% wage growth), now, instead of $1M, we end at $1.75M.

The last part of this equation is the employer retirement contributions we discussed in this section. You may likely have a 401(k) at work where if you put in a certain percentage, your employer will also put in a certain percentage, up to a limit. This is called an employer match—free money (that is the best kind!). Not taking advantage of free money is like not accepting a free ice cream cone that makes you live longer. When we factor in this last piece (3% match, again growing at 5% with your wages), we end at almost $2.3M. Translate that into the 4% rule of thumb, and we have an income stream of around $90,000/yr. That is quite the financial battery.

The ability to have jumps in income, material growth in the financial energy you create, the flexibility to direct where it goes, and free money in the form of employer matches are the advantages of the Matching Arena.

I attempted to choose a middle-of-the-road path example, but there are many variations. If you are an administrator, your income growth may not be as substantial. If you are a president of a company, you may be significantly above this example. The important part here is if you are in this employment arena, you need to save for yourself. The easiest way to do this is to increase your savings rate with your income and make sure your company provides a retirement contribution match. If you allow your pinwheel to get too large and do not have your savings grow with your income, you may very well find yourself with a battery too small to power your pinwheel needs.

Matching Arena Overview

Description: Those jobs working as an employee of a company, with generally higher income potential and employer retirement matching as their primary benefits. Examples include administrators, executives, and other business employees.

Advantages

- Generally, higher income potential through promotions and changing firms.
- Higher income provides the possibility of a larger Financial Pinwheel.
- Higher income allows greater opportunity for saving.
- Saving combined with company matching creates greater wealth possibilities.

Disadvantages

- Majority of the retirement burden is self-managed.
- Higher income may result in an unsustainably large Financial Pinwheel.
- No forced savings to keep on track.

The Entrepreneurial Arena[IP]

I once was on a trip to Fort Lauderdale with my family, a city on the Atlantic side of Florida on the intercoastal.

They had a water taxi ride that brought you up and down the waterway for restaurants and shopping, as well as a narrated tour of the properties along the way. At one point, the guide remarked how we were leaving "Millionaires Row" and entering "Billionaires Row," where the properties went from extraordinarily nice to magnificently remarkable. One house was designed to look like it came out of Harry Potter. Another was reportedly worth around $35M and took up multiple property lots. The yacht parked in front of it was worth $40M, even more than the house itself.

As the guide pointed out the different properties, who lived there, and their stories, I kept a mental tally. It seemed that around 90% of the homes in "Billionaires Row" were owned by what I would classify as entrepreneurs. These were people who owned their firms or had built up their own companies and sold them, mixed in with a few CEOs and celebrities.

There is a reason entrepreneurship is the most famous of all the arenas, often romanticized and certainly glorified. While it has the highest ceiling of all the arenas of employment, it also has the lowest floor. It covers a huge variety of industries—every single company, large or small, is owned by someone. We all know entrepreneurs, such as Mark Zuckerberg or Bill Gates, but the majority of entrepreneurs are all around us. Your accountant who has their own practice is an entrepreneur. The local coffee shop and those million landscaper trucks going up and down every suburban area have owners, as well. Every local business you enter. Even my firm of ten employees makes me an entrepreneur.

This is not the arena we are generally trained for in school. School is geared towards producing for the majority of the employment needs—time-for-money workers. Entrepreneurship is not time-for-money work. You may work 80 hours per week and earn very little or work very little and have a company that earns very much.

When I was young, I pictured myself in the Matching Arena. As life turned out, I wound up in the Entrepreneurial Arena, and I love it. Freedoms of time, purpose, and creativity are now ones that I cannot imagine operating without. At the same time, I had to learn to manage a number of frustrations, pitfalls, and difficulties, and I received entrepreneurial coaching through a firm named Strategic Coach® to make it a journey I could enjoy.

Entrepreneurs have employees to manage, bills to pay, and taxes to file. Many work well in excess of the standard 40-hour work week because it all comes down to them. If the company makes more money, they can make more money. If the company makes less money, they make less money. If the company goes out of business, their income goes to zero. They receive no pension. No one is giving them free matching money into their 401(k). While you are first in line for success, you are also first in line for failure. It isn't easy, often requiring additional planning—it takes a specific type of mentality. That is why it is not for everyone, which is okay; there are three arenas in which we can choose to operate. That doesn't mean you can't leverage ownership in other ways, as you will see in the investment-related chapters. As we build our wind machines, this is just one of the approaches toward building a perpetual pinwheel.

The advantages are pretty clear: the highest income potential, determining your own schedule, and flexibility to build and create as you will. You may also have certain tax advantages, with the business often absorbing some expenses, whether transportation, gas, or other items. If your car qualifies, for example, that payment is a tax-deductible expense for the business. A $500 car payment may turn into only

$350 after accounting for tax savings. When others make their car payment, it is with after-tax funds. So, they may need to earn $650, and after taxes, wind up with $500, which they then use to make the payment.

The disadvantages are less discussed. As already mentioned, there is no pension. There is no free money in the form of retirement matching. You need to save 100% of your retirement funding outside of your government pension (social security). You need to build that financial battery all by yourself.

What makes this saving even more difficult is that many businesses put a large portion of their profits back into the company. It makes sense as the business takes on a personalization, the identity of the owner, and they want it to grow and succeed. At the same time, this leaves less available to build your financial batteries. If the company is sold for a huge profit down the road, then it all likely works out, but many businesses do not operate in this manner. Small landscaping businesses have little to no end-of-life value. Independent attorneys, as well. In my industry, the payout may be just 2–3 years' worth of annual revenue. Certainly, it is not a large enough financial battery contribution to last the rest of your life. If you do not save enough separately, all your eggs are in the eventual sale value bucket.

It is also very difficult to determine the size of your pinwheel. You have a strong January and net $10,000. You have a poor February and net only $5,000. Your cash flow is often quite variable, so having a clear idea of how big your pinwheel is can be challenging. This is why I provided an annualized approach in the Measuring Your Pinwheel section. If your income is variable, then your spending is likely variable too.

A very useful strategy in managing a variable cash flow is to pay yourself a fixed salary. I call this the Variable Pinwheel

Funnel[IP]. Every month, all the income comes into one bank account (all income account) for the business, but then you pay yourself a fixed amount into your personal spending account, similar to any other employee. This way, no matter if there is a good month, a bad month, or something in between, you are always living on the same amount. You know the size of your pinwheel. At the end of the financial year for the company, you can see how much excess built up in the all income account. You can then determine how much additional to save towards yourself, building up those financial batteries, and how much you may want to use on additional spending, increasing the size of your pinwheel, or reinvesting back into the business.

This can be useful in any variable income situation, whether that be the Entrepreneurial Arena or someone in a Hybrid Arena position, such as sales, where there are higher variable commissions.

Variable Pinwheel Funnel[IP]

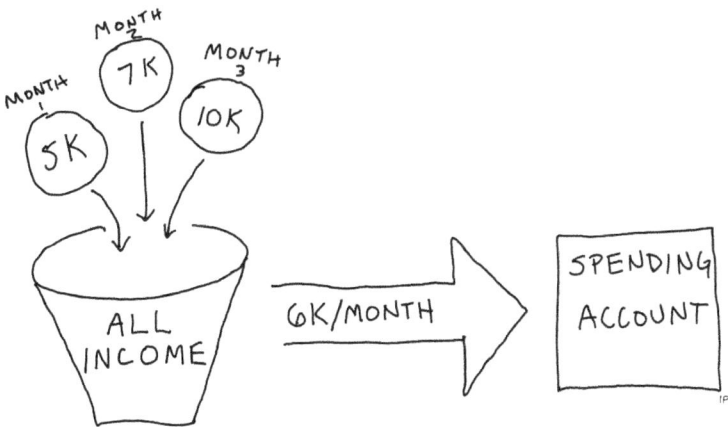

Real estate investing is one of the most often spoken about ventures we hear in the entrepreneurial arena, so I wanted to mention it here specifically. There is a never-ending list of gurus who can help you purchase real estate to great success. HGTV has a new show out every month, it seems, flipping houses or renting them out to great profits. While there are many people who have obviously done very well with these strategies, in my personal experience, our clients, overall, have had minimal success. Managing your home is difficult enough; managing additional properties and those needs can be an outright headache. If you pay a separate managing firm to handle that for you, it also eats into your profits. Managing firms only exist because there are that many people who find self-managing to be too difficult.

Additionally, a reserve needs to be kept for when the furnace goes or months when you can't rent out the property. While the national long-term average home value growth is around 4%,[9] this is extremely dependent on location, and you will give up the opportunity for traditional investment growth on any funds put into the property. If you put down $100,000, for example, into the home, those funds now cannot be invested elsewhere. This all needs to be part of the discussion and equation when determining if this is a direction someone wants to go in. On paper, it is straightforward: have the rent exceed the mortgage, then reap the profits when selling an appreciated property, or net all the rental income when the mortgage runs out. Be aware, though, that understanding the general approach is different than having the level of expertise to execute it. So, is it possible to be successful in real estate? Absolutely. At the same time, it is certainly not as simple as it sometimes seems.

Entrepreneurial Arena Overview

Description: Those who own their own company in any field, where higher profits directly correlate to higher income and lower profits directly correlate to lower income. Examples include accountants, landscapers, or anyone else who owns their own business.

Advantages

- Generally, the highest income potential of any arena.
- Income opportunity provides the possibility for the largest Financial Pinwheel.
- Direct control of time and schedule.
- Depending on the industry, the sale of a company could be a material opportunity.

Disadvantages

- Income goes down directly if the company does poorly.
- Retirement burden is fully self-managed.
- Variable income can lead to a difficult pinwheel to measure and track.
- No forced savings to keep on track, with profits many times reinvested into the company, so the greatest degree of savings self-discipline is required.

Notable Hybrid Arenas

There are a few occupations that sit somewhat between the various arenas and deserve separate acknowledgment. These may enjoy the higher income potential of the Matching Arena with the guaranteed retirement benefits of the Pension Arena or perhaps have more income potential within their control, like in the Entrepreneurial Arena, but there are still some Matching Arena benefits.

Pension and Matching Arena Hybrids

Examples here may include certain unionized trade occupations, such as electricians, as well as union jobs having a higher risk of injury, such as police officers, firefighters, and excavators, where greater compensation is required for the risk entailed. Lastly, high-level c-suite executives would also fall here, where both may be provided to maximize compensation for key personnel.

For the unionized examples, the trend seems to be a transition toward the Matching Arena in many ways. While pensions are still a part of the calculation, they are not as substantial, and require more years in order to obtain them. This results in an additional gap, requiring savings and building up of financial batteries to some degree, where it previously may have never been needed.

Entrepreneurial and Matching Arena Hybrids

The main example here is a sales position. We have some clients where commission income can be 50–90% of their income. The more they sell, the more they make; the less they sell, the less they make, just like in the Entrepreneurial

Arena, and may benefit in utilizing the Variable Pinwheel Funnel. However, they likely don't have the staffing and running a business type responsibilities as in the Matching Arena. If they do have a base salary, again as part of the Matching Arena, they likely receive an employer match on that portion of their income.

Part 1 Recap: Creating a Breeze

1.   Measure Your Pinwheel

Remember, it all has to go somewhere, either saved or spent.

My household take-home pay is:
_____ (ex: 10,000/mo)

My savings *after receiving my take-home pay* are:
_____ (ex: 1,000/mo)

The size of my Financial Pinwheel is:
_____ (ex: 9,000/mo)

Note: For those who may have more variable income, whether through larger commissions, business flows, or otherwise, it may be easier to measure annually. For example, $120,000/yr take-home pay and $12,000/yr saved from that take-home pay, so a $108,000/yr sized pinwheel.

2.   Determine Your Arena of Employment

The Pension Arena

Description: Those jobs receive a pension and job security as their primary benefits. Examples include teachers, postal employees, and other government workers.

Advantages

- Pension provides future guaranteed income
- Social security provides higher % coverage of future needs
- Modest income limits lifestyle expenses = Manageable Pinwheel
- Hard not to stay on track if you put in the time

Disadvantages

- Income opportunity is likely much more limited
- Discretionary spending will need to be less
- May not support the size of desired Financial Pinwheel

The Matching Arena

Description: Those jobs working as an employee of a company, with generally higher income potential and employer retirement matching as their primary benefits. Examples include administrators, executives, and other business employees.

Advantages

- Generally, higher income potential through promotions and changing firms.
- Higher income provides the possibility of a larger Financial Pinwheel.

- Higher income allows greater opportunity for saving.
- Saving combined with company matching creates greater wealth possibilities.

Disadvantages

- Majority of the retirement burden is self-managed.
- Higher income may result in an unsustainably large Financial Pinwheel.
- No forced savings to keep on track.

The Entrepreneurial Arena

Description: Those who own their own company in any field, where higher profits directly correlate to higher income, and lower profits directly correlate to lower income. Examples include accountants, landscapers, or anyone else who owns their own business.

Advantages

- Generally, the highest income potential of any arena.
- Income opportunity provides the possibility for the largest Financial Pinwheel.
- Direct control of time and schedule.
- Depending on the industry, the sale of a company could be a material opportunity.

Disadvantages

- Income goes down directly if the company does poorly.
- Retirement burden is fully self-managed.
- Variable income can lead to a difficult pinwheel to measure and track.
- No forced savings to keep on track, with profits many times reinvested into the company, so the greatest degree of savings self-discipline is required.

Notable Hybrid Arenas

There are a few occupations that sit somewhat between these main three arenas that are worth mentioning.

Pension and Matching Arena Hybrid

These may enjoy the higher income potential of the Matching Arena with the guaranteed retirement benefits of the Pension Arena.

- Certain unionized trade occupations (electricians, plumbers)
- Certain high-risk unionized occupations (police officer, firefighter, excavator)
- Certain c-suite executives

Entrepreneurial and Matching Arena Hybrid

These may enjoy a higher level of income possibility, both positive and negative, as in the Entrepreneurial Arena, while receiving a matching portion at least on base salary, as in the Matching Arena.

- Sales position

Self-guided planning systems can be found at
TheFinancialPinwheel.com

PART 2

Managing the Flow

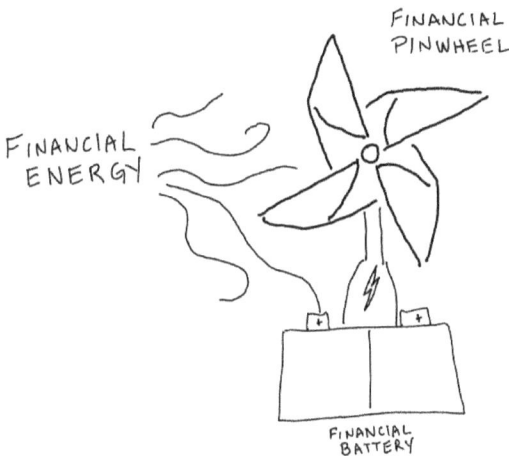

FINANCIAL PINWHEEL

FINANCIAL ENERGY

FINANCIAL BATTERY

A Little Goes a Long Way

A little girl is dancing up and down the edge of the beach after a storm. Her movements are irregular as she bends up and down, casting her arm out here and there towards the ocean. Moving closer to the girl, you can see she is dancing among thousands of starfish that have been washed ashore during the storm. She bends down gracefully with a smile, picks one up, and casts it back into the sea.

She is asked, "Girl, why do you waste your time throwing a few starfish back? There are starfish littered as far as the eye can see. What does it matter? Surely you cannot save them all."

She smiles back, the salt air blowing her hair across her face, as she slowly bends down and casts another soaring into the water. "Well," she says, "it certainly mattered to that one."

Much like the little girl and the starfish, it is not about saving everything. We need to be throwing some starfish back, saving at least a portion of the financial energy we create consistently to build the financial batteries we will need down the road.

If you are in the Pension Arena, the lower end of the income opportunity spectrum, you likely have the least amount of starfish washed up on the beach, but you also do not need to throw as many back.

If you are in the Matching Arena, you have more starfish scattered about, likely more in the way of income, but you also need to throw more back into the water now. You do have some incentives, though, as your employer match essentially is the company helping you throw in a few extra if you first throw in some on your own.

If you are in the Entrepreneurial Arena, your beach may be scattered with the most starfish one month and very few the next, so making sure you throw enough back when they are there and available is very important. It is all on you to execute.

Starfish left on the shore are spent and gone forever. Those thrown back not only live on for you, but they grow and multiply as they do.

Building the Battery

When automobiles first came out, there was a crank on the front that had to be turned in order to get it started. There were no batteries built in, like there are now, to provide the initial energy required.

A financial battery is like any other battery; it stores energy that can be used later. Your financial battery has two separate terminals: the "you" terminal and the "them" terminal[IP]. One is powered by pensions, whether that be corporate or government—so "them." The other is powered by savings—so "you."

The terminal powered by "them" is the social security and pension cell. They may force you to make contributions from your paycheck, but they are being managed, calculated, and funded by them at the end of the day.

When you have excess financial energy, it can go into the savings terminal, being stored for later use. It can be put in a bank account, a retirement plan at work, a non-retirement investment account (Joint/Individual), or anywhere else. Where it is put determines how it may be taxed in the future and how much it can grow, but just putting it away at all is charging the battery.

The YOU Battery Cell

You may already have, or have heard of, many different types of financial battery components that can be used: 401(k)s, IRAs, Roth IRAs, CDs, Bank Accounts, or other investment accounts. These can play a role and are organized into three main battery cells, each with a different goal: Protection, Flexibility, and Growth.

In the protection cell, you can get to the energy at any time, and it stays safe but doesn't grow very much. In the growth cell, the energy has the opportunity to grow on itself, with tax incentives to direct financial energy into it, but it is restricted as to when you may be able to access it and penalties if you disobey. The flexibility cell falls between these two extremes, providing ready access at any time and the opportunity to grow on itself, but no tax incentives for energy added.

You can see for each cell's advantages; you need to give something up in return. If you want safety and access (protection), you give up growth potential and tax incentives. If you want growth potential and access (flexibility), you give up safety and tax incentives. If you want growth potential and tax incentives (growth), you lose safety and access.

Protection (Short-term: Bank, CDs, Money Market)

> **Advantages:** Safety for what you put in, can access at any time
>
> **Disadvantages:** Very limited growth, won't keep up with inflation

The protection cell protects what you have. Growth is not the goal. Here, you would have your emergency fund as well as funds for any shorter-term goals.

An emergency fund is for if your water heater breaks or if you lose your job. It should be able to keep your financial pinwheel spinning for 2–6 months. So, from the prior examples, if your pinwheel measures to be $9,000/mo, then you should have $18,000–54,000 as an emergency fund. There is a little flexibility here based on your comfort level and job type. Some clients can't sleep at night without six months' worth of expenses in the bank. Others, I have to convince to even keep two months' worth of expenses. No matter the scenario, you should fall somewhere in this range.

If you are in the Pension Arena, with a very high degree of job security, then you are probably fine on the lower end of this spectrum. If you are in the Entrepreneurial Arena, you may want to be on the upper end, depending on your business. The more potential variability of income, the greater the emergency fund should be.

The only other appropriate funds for the protection cell are those earmarked for shorter-term goals, such as an upcoming down payment on a house, a car, or a new driveway. Again, in these scenarios, the goal is keeping what we have, not growth.

Any financial energy available above this should always go into one of the next two cells, as storing funds in this protection cell above what is needed actually loses money. How can you lose money if these funds are protected? It is the protection cell, after all, right?

The answer is inflation, the headwinds to your Financial Pinwheel. Generally speaking, the interest rates you receive from the bank are directly influenced by inflation. As inflation goes up, interest rates go up. So, if inflation is at 5%, interest rates may be close to 5%. You pay tax on the interest you receive from the bank, though, so you are netting less than 5%, let's say 4%. If expenses go up at 5% and your bank funds go up at 4%, you essentially are losing money.

Protection Cell Calculation[IP]

My pinwheel measured: _____ (Ex: 9,000/mo)

My emergency fund
goal is: _____ (Ex: 9,000/mo x
4 = 36,000)

My additional short-term
funding is: _____ (Ex: 10,000 Roof
next month)

My Total Protection
Cell Need is: _____ (Ex: 36,000 +
10,000 = 46,000)

My Total Bank funds
currently: _____ (Ex: 60,000)

My Current Excess/
Deficit is: _____ (Ex: 14,000)

How is your protection cell currently situated? This is one of the digital tools that can be found at TheFinancial-Pinwheel.com.

Flexibility (Intermediate-term: Joint or Individual Investment Account)

> **Advantages:** Can access at any time, opportunity for growth
>
> **Disadvantages:** No tax incentives, funds can lose value

While the protection cell is great for protecting what you have, the pinwheel headwinds of inflation make it a poor place to build out any more of your financial battery than needed.

The flexibility cell, as with the growth cell to follow, however, has the opportunity to outpace these headwinds. Here, you may be able to achieve annualized long-term returns of 6–10%, something we will get into in more detail in the subsequent chapter on A Self-Charging Wind Machine.

Overall, it is one of the most important cells while simultaneously being the one most often ignored. This cell uses joint or individual registrations (just like your bank accounts) to simply make them investment accounts that aren't specifically designated for retirement purposes. The investments available in the flexibility or growth cells are essentially the same; it is the type of account you are using that makes it fall into one or the other.

For example, you can have Apple stock in a Joint account or an IRA (Individual Retirement Account). Let's say your

Apple stock was purchased for $100 and goes up to $150. If it is in a Joint Account, you can sell it and withdraw the funds whenever you want. You will have to pay tax on any gains generated ($150 - $100 = $50 gain), but there are no penalties. The tax you pay also depends on your capital gains rate, which is likely much lower than your income tax rate.

If you sold and withdrew the Apple stock from your IRA, all $150 would be taxable as ordinary income. You also are not allowed to withdraw until age 59 ½; otherwise, there is a 10% penalty. So, if you needed extra funds for a home renovation, college, or anything else, you would lose perhaps 40% to taxes and penalties for taking it from an IRA early.

You can see how useful this flexibility cell can be because life can be variable and unexpected. In order to accurately meet these needs, you need to have flexible funds but still have the opportunity to grow.

A good target for this cell is 1–2x your annual income, but this can vary depending on your goals and where you are in life. If retirement is your sole focus, then unless you plan on retiring early before you can access your retirement accounts (as early as 55 for current 401(k)s, but generally 59½), then this cell can likely be on the smaller side. If you are younger, though, and have goals of education for children, a second property, retiring early, or pretty much anything else, then having this cell be more substantial could likely be more appropriate for you.

Growth (Long-term: 401(k), IRA, Roth IRA)

Advantages: Opportunity for growth, tax incentives

Disadvantages: Limited access, funds can lose value

The growth cell is the one we are most familiar with as a place to direct financial energy. It is for long-term growth and is retirement-focused. It is where the matching occurs for those in the Matching Arena. Like the flexibility cell, this one also has the opportunity for growth, with annualized long-term returns perhaps falling somewhere in the 6–10% range if invested appropriately.

Every account here is retirement-focused. Because the government knows their pension social security won't be enough to power our Financial Pinwheels once we stop working, they provide tax incentives to encourage us and our employers to direct financial energy here.

There are two types of incentivized accounts: those that provide a tax deduction and those that grow tax-free (Roth). If you see the word Roth, it means it grows tax-free. If you don't see the word Roth, it means you receive a tax deduction, barring very few exceptions, and you will need to pay tax when you withdraw in retirement.

For example, if I put $100 into my IRA, I receive a $100 tax deduction. I may save $25 in taxes for that year because of my contribution. When I retire, that $100 may have grown to $500. Now, when I withdraw it, all $500 is taxable as income. I may have to pay $125 in taxes on this eventual distribution. Your company match is generally directed here as well since the company wants to receive a tax deduction for their contribution—that is their incentivization.

If we went through the same example, but now I put it into a Roth IRA, there is no tax deduction, so I don't save $25 now. However, that $100 I put in would still grow to $500, and now it is tax-free coming out in retirement, so I am saving $125 in taxes versus the IRA upon distribution. A Roth IRA is like taxing the small seeds instead of the larger harvest down the road, and that is why it is preferred overall, in my opinion.

The first argument against utilizing the Roth primarily is that if you reinvest the $25 tax savings from the IRA scenario, it will make up for the tax savings of the Roth later on. While mathematically accurate, I have never once seen someone in the real world calculate the IRA tax savings out of their annual tax refund and put an additional contribution into their Joint investment account because of it. From a behavioral finance perspective, it makes no sense.

The second argument is that spending in retirement is going to be lower than during someone's working years. While your grandparents may have been content with retiring and relaxing on the front porch for the rest of their lives, our clients now want to retire with the same or often more spending ability to vacation and enjoy life in retirement. Their Financial Pinwheels are the same or larger.

Lastly, the assumption is that tax rates will stay the same. Based on government spending at the moment, many would agree higher tax rates in the future are certainly a possibility at the very least.

The last disadvantage of non-Roth savings is that larger tax refunds usually just expand your lifestyle, making your pinwheel larger. You essentially use the tax refund incentives to subsidize more spending.

Let's say your IRA savings allows you to receive an extra $1,000 in your tax refund. If you are like most people, you will spend this "free" money. You may use it on a vacation every year. A new TV. Remember, all financial energy either goes to your financial battery (savings) or a larger pinwheel to support (spending). If you spend the $1,000 in additional tax savings, increasing the size of your pinwheel, how did the IRA tax deduction really help you financially?

While this cell is the cornerstone of powering our perpetual pinwheel in retirement, it is not the only one that needs attention, especially with its limited flexibility and access during the journey of getting there.

Continuing the exercise from the prior protection cell, how much do you have in each area? This is one of the digital tools that can be found at TheFinancialPinwheel.com.

Flexibility Cell Calculation[IP]

My Total Bank
funds currently: _____ (Ex: $60,000)

My Current
Excess is: _____ (Ex: $14,000)

My Total
Flexibility Cell: _____ (Ex: Joint Investment $50,000)

My Total non-Roth
Growth Cell: _____ (Ex: IRA $150,000, 401k $250,000)

My total Roth
Growth Cell: _____ (Ex: Roth IRA $100,000)

You should now have a good idea of how your current financial batteries are situated and what cells you are using toward building them.

Notable Exception: Education (529 Plans)

Advantages: Opportunity for growth, tax incentives

Disadvantages: Limited Access, funds can lose value

As not everyone has education savings as a goal, it isn't one of the core three cells. If you do have education as a goal, this cell may be appropriate to utilize. If you notice, it has the same advantages and disadvantages as the Growth cell. This is because, just like retirement, the government is trying to incentivize you to save for education needs.

529 Plans grow tax-free if it is used for qualified education expenses. This can be private high schools, colleges, or even trade schools. Uncle Jimmy's backyard garage courses are not going to count; however, most legitimate education-related expenses will be covered. Every state has its own 529 plan, which, in some cases, can provide additional state tax incentives or deductions. No matter which one you use, the growth is tax-free for education, so if there are no tax advantages in your state plan, feel free to look at outside-state plans as well.

The main limitations here are in the access and flexibility. If you do not use the funds for education, for example, if your child received a full scholarship and you instead wanted to use the 529 Plan funds for their wedding, there would be the same retirement 10% penalty and taxes on the growth.

You are allowed to change the beneficiary; maybe your oldest received a scholarship and didn't need the funds, so it can be moved to another child, individual, or even yourself. Despite this flexibility, many families we work with mentally consider those 529 funds to be for that specific child, so they aren't always comfortable using this changing beneficiary option.

The only other flexibility comes in the ability to use a portion of the funds towards a Roth IRA for the child, to a certain degree. For example, if your child didn't use $10,000 of their 529 Plan upon graduation, you could use these funds towards a Roth IRA contribution for them. It still has to fall under the annual contribution limits (if the annual limit is $7k, they can't put all $10k in during one year), the 529 had to be open for at least 15 years, and there is a lifetime maximum as well. As you can see, this provides some flexibility, but a large leftover will likely not be able to be utilized fully.

Much like an airplane mask, I recommend putting your mask on first prior to assisting children with education needs. Your financial batteries should already be on track to power your own pinwheel. Remember that you can always borrow for education, but you cannot borrow for retirement. While you may not want your children to have school loans, you can always help them in making the payments as they build up their careers, if you like, which is much easier than putting out tens of thousands of dollars upfront.

If you complete The Pinwheel Multiplier exercise later in this chapter, for example, and you are on track but still feel like you can save a higher percentage, then great. It seems like you likely have room to save into a 529 Plan.

There is no right or wrong when it comes to education goals. I see most people want to mimic what was provided to them. I personally had some help for college but also came away with manageable loans. I thought this was great as it taught me responsibility and built up my credit. My wife, on the other hand, was fortunate enough to have her college fully covered, walking away with no debt. As a result, she was able to start saving much earlier than I was, and she really appreciated the head start. We each have a tendency to duplicate our own experiences with our children.

The most prudent approach is first determining if education expenses are likely to happen in your situation. If they are, then next is putting birthday or gift money into a 529 Plan for the child. Finally, if you are confident in being on the correct path yourself, then you can afford to add some more to their cell as well. Remember that the Flexibility cell above can also be used for education needs. That is the beauty of the Flexibility cell: those funds can be used for anything.

We often use only the Flexibility cell when children are young, then lump sum fund a 529 plan when the child is a bit older, and the parents have a better idea of what direction they may be heading. Each parent can contribute 5x the annual gifting limit all at once. If the gifting limit is $15,000, it would be $15,000 x 5 x 2 parents = $150,000. If you do this when the child is, say, eight years old, the funds may double by the time they are 18 years old to $300,000. $150,000 in tax-free education growth would have been generated in this example.

Compounding Your Catch

Once you are meeting your Protection cell needs, any extra starfish you throw back into the sea should be directed into your Flexibility and/or Growth cells. These cells contain investments, holdings that have the opportunity to appreciate much more significantly than what you can receive from the bank.

When the bank takes your money and gives you 5% interest, what do you think they are doing with your money? They are investing it in areas where they can earn more than 5%, of course. You are acting as a loaner, loaning your money to the bank. The bank earns more than the 5% they pay you, making a profit. If they didn't, they wouldn't be in business.

When investing in the Flexibility and Growth cells, you are likely going to be investing mostly as an owner, buying shares of different companies. If you own one share of Apple Stock, you are an owner, albeit a very small owner, of Apple. If Apple does well as a company, its stock will likely appreciate. Your one share of stock now is worth more than it was before.

If you invest most of your money as a loaner, you may receive only 5% long-term. Compared to someone who invests most of their money as an owner, they may earn perhaps 7% or more long-term. It may not seem like much of a difference, but someone saving 500/mo for 30 years would have an additional almost 50% at the end of the term—around $610,000 versus $415,000—with those few additional percentages of annual return.

This is compound interest, money growing on itself. It is the most powerful tool you have, and the more time you have, the more you can leverage it. Those starfish you throw back don't just hang around doing nothing. They reproduce: 10 starfish turn into 20 starfish, 20 into 40, 40 into 80, 80 into 160, and on and on they go. The more time they have, the more starfish that get made. Each successive double is exponentially greater than the last.

How Much to Save Mr. Grasshopper

When determining how much to save, the first consideration is what arena of employment you are in. This determines how much in the way of pensions can be used to power your pinwheel down the road.

Remember the other grasshopper from the fable? It is not about saving everything like the ant or saving nothing like the first grasshopper. It is about saving the right amount for yourself first at the beginning of the day, freeing up the rest of your financial energy to do as you please.

There is a doubling relationship between what you save and what you spend. If you save $100, then you are also living on $100 less, so $200 in your favor. Your financial battery became $100 larger, and your financial pinwheel became $100 smaller. A bigger battery and an easier pinwheel to spin.

If you spend $100 more, then you are also saving $100 less, so $200 against you. Your battery is now $100 less than it could have been, and your financial pinwheel became $100 larger. The battery is smaller, and the pinwheel is harder to spin. It is either two positives for you or two negatives against you, as detailed earlier in Part I.

Financial Energy Flow Tradeoff[IP]

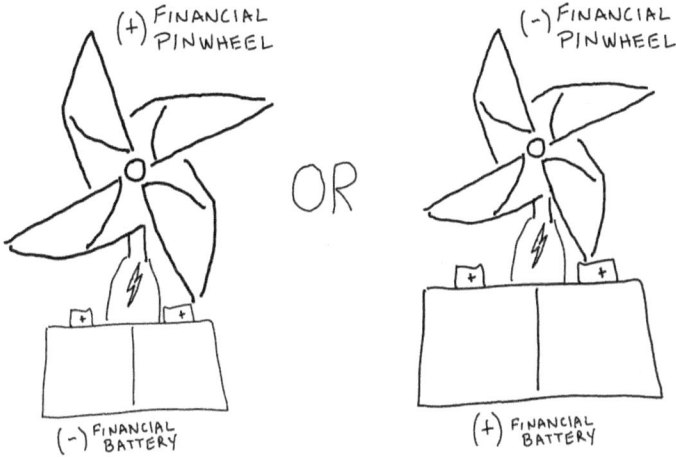

Pension Arena Savings

If you are in the Pension Arena, your "them" terminal is much bigger. Because of this, saving 5–10% of your income will most likely be sufficient for your future needs.

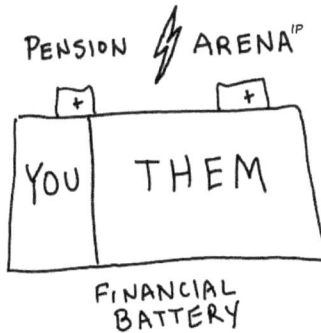

It will not be enough to pay for expensive college educations or second vacation homes, but it will provide you with enough flexibility to handle the unexpected expenses for life down the road. This, again, is the big advantage of the Pension Arena. You have less disposable income, but it keeps your pinwheel much more manageable, and you do not have to think as much about savings to get to retirement.

Matching Arena Savings

If you are in the Matching Arena, your "you" terminal is much bigger. You may need to save 10–15% if you start young (before age 35) and 20–30% or more if you start later in life. There is some help, though, with the employer contributing anywhere from 3–5% of the required contribution. A good general target is 20%.

If you save at the higher end of what you are capable of, simultaneously keeping your pinwheel to a manageable size, you may very well have the ability to contribute materially to college educations, purchase a second home down the road, or even retire earlier. You have more to manage independently, but the possibilities are more flexible.

Entrepreneurial Arena Savings

The Entrepreneurial Arena is the hardest, as there is no match, and there is a pull to put profits back into the business, limiting saving. If you do not expect you will be able to sell your future business for any material amount—and here you should be very honest with yourself, considering like businesses and what they have sold for—then it would be similar to the Matching Arena above, saving 15% if starting young, and 20–35% or more depending how late you start past that in life.

Think of it this way: If you start saving young, it is like putting a marble in your pocket—minimally annoying. You don't love it, but you quickly get used to it, soon not even realizing it is there. This is similar to small, consistent deposits into your financial battery over a long period of time.

If you wait a bit before you start saving, now you have to shove a baseball in your pocket. Maybe it's still doable, but not really comfortable. Your financial battery needs more sizable deposits to build up sufficiently, but you can do it.

If you wait too long, you reach the point where you need to shove a basketball in your pocket. This is a virtually impossible struggle that will require significant pinwheel alterations to complete or, more likely, require you to work longer, generating more financial energy so that your battery has more time to charge up and a shorter time to power your perpetual pinwheel.

So, what percent are you currently saving? Take the amount you are saving and divide by your gross (pre-tax) income. We use gross income here, including your employer's work plan contributions. If you have an employer match, add that in, too, at the end. Remember, if you put money aside but then spend it later on vacations, car repairs, or any other expense, it does not count as savings.

I have a full example here to start, as the matching percentage for those in that arena can be a bit confusing to incorporate. Remember that TheFinancialPinwheel.com has full video guides with calculators that you can utilize to assist.

	Individual	Spouse (if applicable)	
Monthly Savings	1,000	700	(ex: 200 Joint + 800 401k = 1k/mo)
Gross Income	12,500	10,000	(ex: 12,500/mo)
Percent Saved	8%	7%	(ex: 1,000 / 12,500 = 8%)
Employer Match	3%	5%	(ex: 3%)
Saving Rate %	11%	12%	(ex: 8% + 3% = 11%)
Household Savings	1,700		(ex: 1,000 + 700)
Household Match $	875		(ex: 3% x 12,500 + 5% x 10,000)
Household Total	2,575		(ex: 1,700 + 875)
Household Gross Inc.	22,500		(ex: 12,500 + 10,000)
Household Savings %	11.44%		(ex: 2,575 / 22,500)

	Individual	Spouse (if applicable)	
Monthly Savings			(ex: 200 Joint + 800 401k = 1k/mo)
Gross Income			(ex: 12,500/mo)
Percent Saved			(ex: 1,000 / 12,500 = 8%)
Employer Match			(ex: 3%)
Saving Rate %			(ex: 8% + 3% = 11%)
Household Savings			(ex: 1,000 + 700)
Household Match $			(ex: 3% x 12,500 + 5% x 10,000)
Household Total			(ex: 1,700 + 875)
Household Gross Inc.			(ex: 12,500 + 10,000)
Household Savings %			(ex: 2,575 / 22,500)

How do you feel about how many starfish you are currently throwing, or not throwing, back in?

Credit Card Debt and Savings

If you are saving into investment accounts but have nagging credit card debt, then your savings are more of a mirage. While taking advantage of an employer matching amount may still make sense, as even a 50% match is still a 50% return on your investment, anything above that should be directed towards debt payoff first. Saving into an investment and receiving maybe 7–10% versus paying off a credit card that is charging you 20% interest means you are losing money at the end of the day. Pay off your debt, then save.

The Pinwheel Multiplier – How Big Should Your Battery Be?

When I work with clients, I can use advanced software that maps out precise cash flows, incorporating when certain debts like a mortgage end, exact social security payments, pensions, build-in educational expenses, second homes, downsizing in retirement—so pretty much everything and anything—and stress test the whole scenario in a Monte Carlo simulation. I can tell them if they are on track or behind where they should be. Obviously, in the scope of this book, that is not plausible, but many of you may want to go deeper than just a general savings rate needed at various age ranges.

Most of what you will find as guidance online utilizes your age and income to estimate if you are on track. While simple, it does not factor in how much of that income you are actually spending, meaning the size of your pinwheel. Someone making $100,000 saving 20% doesn't need as much saved today as a person making that same amount but only saving 5%. The first person has a smaller pinwheel and a greater percentage of financial energy going into their batteries. As a result, they need less saved up today.

This exercise is most helpful if you are in the Matching or Entrepreneurial Arena. (The Pension Arena is pretty straightforward: a 5–10% savings rate for most of your working career is likely sufficient.)

While it cannot obviously take into account the intricacies of your situation, it may be able to give you a general idea if what you have saved appears to be sufficient based on your current savings rate.

The goal of this exercise is not to definitively tell if you have built up enough at this point. The goal is to gauge if you likely should try and increase your savings or if you may have flexibility to enjoy more today.

If you and your spouse are both in the Matching and/ or Entrepreneurial Arenas, you can complete this exercise cumulatively. If one spouse is in the Pension Arena, you can exclude their portion and focus only on the income from the other spouse.

All you need is your Annual Pinwheel and the multiplier table below based on your age. This is based on a 30 year retirement. This may seem long to some, and perhaps too short for others with family longevity, but we would rather have a little too much than not enough. Again, this is one of the digital tools available through the self-guided planning systems at TheFinancialPinwheel.com.

	Pinwheel Multiplier[IP]	
Age	**Standard**	**High Income (500k)**
30	1.50	2.25
35	2.00	3.00
40	3.50	5.25
45	5.00	7.50
50	6.50	9.75
55	8.00	12.00
60	10.00	15.00
65	12.50	18.75

If your Annual Pinwheel is $108,000 ($9,000/mo), you can see roughly how much you probably should have saved into your financial batteries at different points.

Age 30 = 162,000   (1.5 x 108,000)
Age 50 = 702,000   (6.5 x 108,000)
Age 65 = 1,350,000 (12.5 x 108,000)

Again, if you are a bit below where you are calculated to be, that is fine. Remember that this is for a 30 year retirement. If you want to still be able to retire for this length, you now know you should likely be increasing your savings rate. If further savings are not possible for you, then a shorter retirement would require less currently saved. A shorter retirement could mean for some that you may have to work a little longer or take on a part-time job in retirement, which can go a long way. Working one extra year or part-time for a few years can reduce the strain on your Financial Batteries by tens of thousands of dollars. For example, working part-time for five years and earning just $30,000 is $150,000 less that your Financial Batteries will have to replace

Alternatively for others, they may feel that a 20 year retirement is more appropriate based on family longevity. Again here, they would not need to hit the multiplier exactly. As a general rule of thumb though, you probably want to be reaching at least 60% of the calculated result to ensure you have a solid base. At least you better know now what you need to do or how you may likely have to adjust.

On the reverse of that, if you are ahead of these numbers, you may likely be on a path where you can retire early or afford additional spending on things you may enjoy. Saving additional for college also becomes more of a possibility.

Lastly, you can see a column for high-income earners. If your household income is on the larger side, then you should be using a larger pinwheel multiplier. The more you earn, the less impact your government pension (social security) income will have for you. Social security has a maximum benefit limit. If you earn $200,000 or $500,000, for example, your social security benefit will be the same. The higher income earner likely has a much larger pinwheel; however, social security will represent a much smaller percentage of coverage for their needs. A larger financial battery is required.

Battery Supercharging Opportunities

In the course of our lives, there are various supercharging opportunities. Some depend on our arena of employment, others are based on luck and circumstance. Either way, being aware of them and viewing them as opportunities instead of just "free" money allows us to take advantage. The biggest key here is having a plan in advance: If one of the following items happens to you, what action do you plan to take? Without a plan in advance, the likelihood of these opportunities being missed and spent instead rises dramatically.

Reduced Expenses

Most expenses go one way, and that way is up, but there are some expenses where that is not the case. When these expenses drop off or decrease, this is a great opportunity to save more for yourself instead of having those funds simply spent elsewhere. Below are a few examples, but it really can be any expense once paid off.

- **Car Payment** – If you pay off a car loan, that may be an extra $100–1,000/mo available to you to now save towards yourself. If you don't have a plan to consciously save your car payment once the loan is done, it will most likely just disappear to other new expenses. This can also be applicable when choosing a new car. If you choose a modest brand versus a luxury brand, for example, it may save you a few hundred dollars per month. An extra $200/mo saved for 30 years at just 7% is roughly an extra $250,000. If you want a luxury brand car, that is certainly fine too. Again, it is not about building the smallest Financial Pinwheel possible; it is about being more intentional about the one you build and understanding the additional savings needed to power it accordingly.
- **Daycare/Childcare** – This is perhaps the single most important expense for younger families to take advantage of ending. It can be well over $1,000/mo,

depending on the area you live. Generally speaking, when children reach a certain age, these expenses either go away or are greatly reduced. If these funds just disappear towards other expenses, however, it is a huge missed opportunity and likely severely detrimental to future abilities to reach goals. An extra $1,000/mo saved for 20 years at just 7% is roughly an extra $520,000.

- **Mortgage Refinance** – A mortgage is generally viewed as good debt. It comparatively has a lower, potentially tax-deductible rate and can be spread over 30 years. If you were to ask me why I have a 30-year mortgage, my answer would be that they don't offer 40-year mortgages.

  A mortgage payment is based on the interest rate, term, and starting value—this last point is very important. A mortgage with a starting value of $300,000 and a current balance of $150,000 will have a payment that is still based on the original $300,000.

  For example, if the mortgage above had an interest rate of 4%, the payment would be around $1,400/mo. If you refinanced the loan at 6%, a 50% higher interest rate, you would actually lower your monthly payment by $500/mo. This is because it would be a new 30-year loan based on the current balance of $150,000, a significantly lower starting value.

  Many find this hard to initially fathom, as they focus only on the interest rate number and interest to be paid. This thought process ignores the opportunity available from the new $500/mo in savings, though. If you saved this, for example, into a Roth

IRA earning 7%, then in 30 years, when your mortgage was over, you would have in excess of $600,000 of tax-free funds available.

I will always have a mortgage because a paid-off home is a buried asset. I can only access the funds if I sell the property. The mortgage allows me to access and leverage that value, providing not only the opportunity for greater growth but also more flexibility in cases where those funds may be needed. If I lost my job and my mortgage was paid off, would saving that $1,400/mo in principal and interest (not taxes and insurance, which are always mandatory) really be enough to keep me in my home? I would rather have an additional $200,000 in investments outside the home, allowing me to better bridge the unemployment gap and helping me avoid an immediate, forced duress situation. The bank will not give you a loan if you have no income.

Despite the supporting mathematics behind it, this strategy, in particular, requires a higher level of emotional comfort and clarity in its approach. Having no mortgage on your home has been a goal taught since the Great Depression, and if you can't sleep at night over it, then it is not worth it. Additionally, if you simply refinance and spend the additional savings, then you are just leveraging your home to artificially support a larger pinwheel—a disastrous approach.

Lump Sum Opportunities

- **Bonus Savings** – This can come in many forms: a bonus from your job, sale of restricted stock (RSUs) or stock options, or even a tax refund. It is a lump sum of money outside of what you normally live on, which makes it extra.

If you spend your bonus income every year, then it is part of your pinwheel—it should be added to the measurement. You receive a $12,000 net bonus. You spend all of it every year on vacations. Your base pinwheel of $9,000/mo based on take-home pay alone then is really a pinwheel of $10,000/mo once you factor in the bonus (12,000 / 12 = 1,000; 9,000 base + 1,000 bonus broken out monthly = 10,000).

Planning in advance is key here. It does not all have to be saved, but at least a material part should likely be. An extra $5,000/yr in bonus, whether that be an actual bonus, tax refund, or anything else, for 25 years at 7% is over $300,000 in additional funds. Even better, if you use it toward your Roth IRA every year, it is $300,000 of tax-free funds.

There is also room here to get creative. I have some clients whose bonus is a large percentage of their income, accounting for 15% or more in some cases. Here, they often find it helpful to say they will save 100% of their bonus, essentially pretending it doesn't even exist and it handles all their annual savings required to meet their goals. They get to live off of 100% of their paycheck and not worry about any monthly savings because their bonus alone meets their annual savings needs.

- **Inheritance** – This can often be a large variable. Parents or grandparents may pass away, leaving material funds to their heirs. If these funds are looked at again simply as "free" money, the inheritance can

quickly be squandered, with little long-term benefits to show for it. If you were to receive $100,000
tomorrow, how much of it would you save? If you
saved $50,000 of it, then in 20 years at 7%, you would
have a little less than $200,000.

The other difficulty here when it comes to inheritance is that we often don't know if and when it
will occur. Sharing finances with children is viewed
as inappropriate many times, but generational planning can be a huge advantage for those who utilize
it. Here, we create plans for efficiently transferring
assets to the next generation while making them
aware of their existence to some degree. If your child
is working hard to save everything they can but is
unaware of a material inheritance they are to receive,
then they may potentially be passing up opportunities like trips to Disney World with young kids,
missing memories they could be making.

Part 2 Recap: Managing the Flow

1. Build Your Battery

There are two terminals in your financial batteries: the "THEM" and the "YOU."

"THEM" = Pensions (government, employer, or otherwise)

"YOU" = Savings Cells (Protection, Flexibility, Growth)

Protection (Short-term: bank, CDs, money market)

- Advantages: Safety for what you put in, can access at any time
- Disadvantages: Very limited growth, won't keep up with inflation

Flexibility (Intermediate-term: Joint or Individual Investment Account)

- Advantages: Can access at any time, opportunity for growth
- Disadvantages: No tax incentives, funds can lose value

Growth (Long-term: 401(k), IRA, Roth IRA)

- Advantages: Opportunity for growth, tax incentives
- Disadvantages: Limited access, funds can lose value

Notable Exception: Education (529 Plans)

- Advantages: Opportunity for growth, tax incentives
- Disadvantages: Limited Access, funds can lose value

2. Calculate Your Savings

Savings Goals

- Pension Arena = 5–10%
- Matching Arena = 20–30% (10–15% under Age 30)
- Entrepreneurial Arena = 20–35% (15% under Age 30)

	Individual	Spouse (if applicable)	
Monthly Savings			(ex: 200 Joint + 800 401k = 1k/mo)
Gross Income			(ex: 12,500/mo)
Percent Saved			(ex: 1,000 / 12,500 = 8%)
Employer Match			(ex: 3%)
Saving Rate %			(ex: 8% + 3% = 11%)
Household Savings			(ex: 1,000 + 700)

Household Match $		(ex: 3% x 12.5k + 5% x 10,000)
Household Total		(ex: 1,700 + 875)
Household Gross Inc.		(ex: 12,500 + 10,000)
Household Savings %		(ex: 2,575 / 22,500)

3. Pinwheel Multiplier

Exercise to see how much you should roughly have today based on your pinwheel size.

	Pinwheel Multiplier	
Age	Standard	High Income (500k)
30	1.00	2.00
35	2.00	3.00
40	3.50	5.25
45	5.00	7.50
50	6.50	9.75
55	8.00	12.00
60	10.00	15.00
65	12.50	18.75

If your Annual Pinwheel is \$108,000 (\$9,000/mo), you can see roughly how much you probably should have saved into your financial batteries at different points.

Age 30 = 162,000   (1.5 x 108,000)

Age 50 = 702,000   (6.5 x 108,000)

Age 65 = 1,350,000   (12.5 x 108,000)

If you are a bit behind, that is fine. You now know you should likely be saving more. If further savings is not possible, you may have to work a little longer or take on a part-time job in retirement. At least you better know now what you may need to do.

> Self-guided planning systems can be found at
> TheFinancialPinwheel.com

PART 3

A Self-Charging Wind Machine

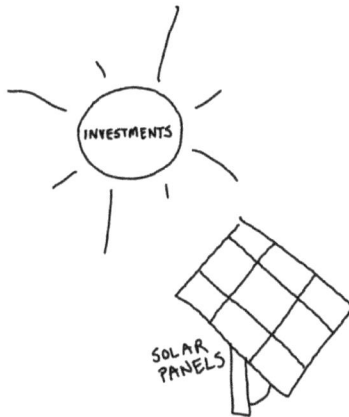

It Takes a Forest

The King Cole Trio recorded the first version of "The Christmas Song" in 1946. The famous first line, "Chestnuuuuuts roasting on an open fiiire..." has been warming the holiday season soundwaves ever since.

You may never have eaten a chestnut, though. Do you know why that probably is? The reason is that by the time this song was written, American chestnut trees, roughly 4 billion of them, had been mostly wiped out by a fungus known as the chestnut blight. American Chestnuts were once a staple of American forests, covering 200 million acres of land and representing 25% of the eastern hardwood forests. Native Americans and the settlers who followed all relied on the up to 6,000 nuts per year each large mature tree could produce.

The blight came and, within 40 years, had spread across the continent, essentially wiping out the species. No more tasty chestnuts. While European imports continued for some time after, by the 1970s, there were virtually no vendors left in New York City.[10]

What would have happened if you had a forest just of American chestnuts? Well, quite simply, you would have lost everything. Not every species of tree is susceptible to every disease, though. Asian chestnut trees, which likely carried the disease over, have a natural resistance to the fungus. Native oak, maple, and pine are unaffected by this fungus as well. Even though one tree struggled, the forest survived.

A forest is a collection of parts, stronger when they are interwoven together than when they are separated out individually. This is the same approach when building your self-charging wind machine through investments. We want to build a forest.

Setting Your DTSI[IP] Expectations

Building your forest comes down to three elements: diversifying, time, and staying invested[IP]. You can remember this as DTSI—you don't want to be ditsy in life, but you do want to be DTSI in investing.

Diversify the Forest

There is no one right way to invest. There are ways to invest that are more likely to keep you on track than others, though.

For starters, think about every investing movie you have ever seen: *Wall Street, Boiler Room, The Wolf of Wall Street.* For however many you've seen, you now have a list of all the ways not to do it. If it is entertaining enough for Hollywood, it is not a practical approach. Your investments are a tool; they are not for entertainment.

One of my hobbies is woodworking. I've built an entryway bench, my dining room table, and the deck off the back of my house, to name a few. To do so, I need tools. A circular saw can cut through a piece of wood with ease. It can also cut right through my finger. You measure twice, cut once, and never put your finger on the trigger until you are ready to start the blade. Every tool needs to be treated with respect. The same applies to the tools used with your Financial Pinwheel.

Investments are solar panels, the tool for self-charging your financial battery. During your working years, they compound your energy to more quickly grow your battery: $125,000 turns into $250,000, $250,000 into $500,000, $500,000 into $1,000,000, and so on, with each successive double yielding exponentially larger results through compounding. When you stop working, they replenish the energy lost by the battery in powering your pinwheel. If your battery continues to be replenished, it can keep spinning your pinwheel perpetually.

Because of their vital importance, your financial battery and solar panels should be structured with care. Buying individual stocks and trying to hit it big is not a repeatable recipe for professional money managers, never mind the average individual. That is why I recommend an approach where you spread out your funds everywhere, all the time—diversifying the forest. No matter how good American chestnuts may seem, we don't want a forest only of them.

In 2007, the legendary investor Warren Buffet challenged hedge funds, betting a million dollars that over a decade, an S&P 500 Index fund would outperform. The S&P 500 Index fund simply holds the 500 largest US companies by size, so there is no special stock picking at all. There was only one hedge fund manager who accepted the challenge. In 2017, the results were not even close, with the index fund trouncing the hedge fund competition.[11] Outperforming for one year—picking a great stock here or there—and doing so repeatedly over the long term are very different things.

We want to spread out our investments even further than just the S&P 500, though, beyond just large US companies. From 2000 to 2009, the S&P 500 index returned -9.10%, annualized to -0.95% per year, in a rare event of losing money over a decade. Fittingly, it became known as the lost decade. The next decade, however, 2010–2019, it grew 256%, annualized to 13.56% per year.

To get an idea of how different areas of the market may move, see the chart below. This chart compares the annualized returns from the S&P 500 Index (large US companies), the Russell 2000 Index (small US companies), and the DJ US Select REIT Index (real estate US companies).

	Annualized Returns by Decade		
	Large US	Small US	Real Estate US
2000 - 2009	-0.95%	3.51%	10.67%
2010 - 2019	13.56%	11.83%	11.57%
2000 - 2019	6.06%	7.59%	11.12%

You may look at this and say, "US Real Estate looks great. That is where I should just put everything! It appears consistently dominant, right?" However, for the first four years in the following decade, 2020–2023, the S&P 500 annualized at over 12%, while US Real Estate was barely over 2%. You really just never know what area is going to do well or poorly over any one period of time. A timespan of ten years may seem like a long time period for us with our lifespans, but for investments, it may just be one single market cycle. You've probably heard of dog years; this is the reverse of that; this is like tree years. Spreading it out everywhere, all the time, again provides that diversification so that we keep moving in the right direction consistently. If we were in, for example, all three of those above areas, we would've moved in the right direction for each time period.

Believe it or not, those three areas above are still only a small selection of different investment areas, referred to formally as asset classes, you can invest in. There are also foreign stocks, emerging markets stocks, government bonds, corporate bonds, and so on and so forth. There is a huge variety of trees we can select from when building our forest.

While variety is great in some respects, it can also be quite daunting. If I were building a real forest from scratch, I would have almost 900 native tree varieties to choose from. Oak trees alone have 90 native varieties. If I expanded to all tree species, that is another 60,000. I'll leave the real forest making to the landscape architects.

This is why, if you are managing your investments individually, I recommend using allocation funds or target-date funds as the most practical approach. These funds cover a broad spectrum of areas—US, foreign, small companies, large companies, etc.—and all you have to do is pick out how conservative or aggressive you want to be. You purchase one fund, and you are instantly spread out over thousands of holdings.

A Target Date fund is a good example here; you likely see these in your company work plans. They stagger every five years, so you pick the one that most closely matches your retirement. If you were going to retire in 2045, then you would pick the 2045 target date fund. It would start out more aggressive, and then as you get closer to 2045, it would slowly get more conservative, assuming you will start needing the money at retirement. 529 Plans have similar options, with your child's age instead of your retirement date being the determining factor of when it is more aggressive or conservative. If your child is 2, you would pick the 0–5 Age-Based Fund. When they turned 6, it would automatically turn into the 6–10 Age-Based Fund, and so on and so forth.

General allocation funds are in the same vein, except they usually are outside of retirement plans. Here, you may see conservative (income), moderate (growth and income), or aggressive (growth) portfolios. These spread out your funds in a similar fashion without the feature of automatically becoming more conservative at some predetermined date.

Overall, whether it be retirement, education, or general investing money, your goal is to consistently go in the right direction over the long term, not to have the highest return out of all your neighbors. Remember, investments are a tool, not a game for entertainment.

Some people just can't help but want to play with a little bit of their investment money. While I do not encourage it, if this is you, then it should be limited to money you can afford to lose, just as if you were to go to a casino. When working with clients, we additionally limit any individual stock or "play" accounts to no more than 15% of their invested assets. The additional flexibility here would be for people who have

A Self-Charging Wind Machine

stock options, restricted stock (RSU), performance stock units (PSU), employee stock ownership plans (ESOP), or the like, where the benefits are granted in company stock. In these examples, when the stock can be sold and subsequently diversified, that is the course we generally recommend taking after any applicable tax considerations.

Tiiiiiime Is on My Side, Yes It Is

As the old saying goes, the best time to plant a tree is 30 years ago. The second best time is today. What you do, and sometimes more importantly what you do not do, over that period is exceedingly important. To help you make the right choices, you should be prepared for what to expect.

Let's say there was a game where if you put in $1,000, there was a 50% chance you would get more than $1,000 back and a 50% chance you would get less than $1,000 back. You very well may not be willing to play this game, as winning and losing have an equal chance.

What if, however, the odds increased so that 75% of the time, you received more than $1,000 back? What about an 85% chance? What about a 95% chance of getting more than $1,000 back? Surely, at 95%, most anyone would feel confident, right?

While diversifying can provide more stability and consistency in returns, this exercise shows the importance of time in the equation. On any one day, historically speaking, there is roughly a 50% chance the market will go up and, therefore, a 50% chance it will go down. Over any one-year period, there is roughly a 75% chance the market will go up. Over any three-year period, there is roughly an 85% chance it will go up. Over any ten-year period, there is roughly a 95% chance it will go up. To date, there has never been a

97

15-year period in which the market was lower than it had started. While every investment disclosure is required to tell you that past performance is no guarantee of future results, that is some pretty extensive history. Ending with more than you started, therefore, becomes an exercise in time more than anything else.

Let's look again at the S&P 500 Index for the same 20-year period from 2000 to 2019. There were five negative years and fifteen positive years, so right on the mark, with 75% of the one-years being positive. Out of the 18 rolling three-year calendar periods, 13 were positive, or 72% of the time, so below long-term averages. Out of the 11 ten-year rolling calendar periods, ten were positive, or 91%, so pretty much right on the mark there as well. Finally, as expected, all six of the rolling fifteen-year periods were also positive, so 100%.

If the market usually goes up, and the longer you wait, the higher the likelihood this will occur; how come people say they lose money? The answer is in the last part of the DTSI equation: staying invested.

Keep the Solar Panel Outside

You're at a traffic light, waiting for the light to change, admiring the blue sky as white clouds slowly float by. The warm sun radiates through the windshield as your favorite song comes on. You turn up the volume and drum along to the beat on the steering wheel. What a wonderful day! Suddenly, your body jolts forward—someone hit the back of your car! Can you believe it? What an idiot! Of all the things, why did it have to happen to you today? It just isn't fair!

The thing is, you rarely meet anyone who has been driving for any considerable amount of time and has never been in any kind of accident. Whether we consciously acknowledge it or not, every time we step into the car, we have the opportunity of an accident happening. Averages show most people have 3 or 4 automobile accidents in a lifetime.[12] For first-year drivers, a staggering 43% are in accidents.[13] You should expect to have 3 or 4 yourself at some point, and your first-year driver is basically a coin flip.

If you are investing, you need to come to terms with what to expect as well. If you don't, you will likely move your money out of the market when it gets stormy, moving your solar panels inside. Your solar panels can't charge if they are inside. If you need money tomorrow, it should be inside where it is safe. We just saw that 50% of the time, any one day in the market could be negative. Even funds that are needed in 1–2 years should likely be inside, safe in a bank money market. Funds that have longer time frames are different, though, and if we don't have our solar panels out and ready to go when the sun comes back out, shining and strong, we miss out on that energy forever.

That is why your expectation from the very start should be that there will be storms. Just like in real life, there is always another storm to come at some point. As crazy as it would be to look up at the sky after a storm and say, "That's probably the last storm I'll ever see in my lifetime," it is equally crazy to look at a recent downturn in the market and say, "This is probably the last time the market will drop." Your accounts will go down at times. Not maybe, not hopefully not; they absolutely will. There is no way around this happening. It has to be consciously accepted from day one. Again, if you look at your accounts every day, 50% of the time, they are going to be down. This is why people who check their performance every day generally have a harder time staying invested and making the right investment decisions. Every storm cloud becomes a concern.

There is an analogy that says investments are like a bar of soap. The more they're touched, the less you have. Am I suggesting not to be aware? Of course not. Wash your hands as needed, stay generally aware, and review for any transaction errors or the like, but washing excessively in the form of constant performance monitoring will likely only inspire ill-advised actions to be taken.

For example, our same 20-year period of 2000–2019 had only five negative years, but their timing, circumstances, and stories around them caused emotions to become entangled with the actions people took with their investments. People had the urge to take their solar panels in with the storm.

Three of the negative years—2000, 2001, and 2002— happened all at once. These were the years following the dot-com bubble burst. After three negative years, each progressively worse, many investors may have said enough is enough and sold off their investments. "This internet thing is a disaster!" they told themselves. "I'll invest again once the market goes back up and things look better." By then, though, it is too late. The next year, it went up 28%. If you were sitting on the sidelines, your solar panels in the shed, then that growth to recoup your losses was missed forever.

Another storm happened in 2008. The Financial Crisis, as it was so forebodingly named, caused an almost 37% drop in the market. "The entire financial system is ruined!" people said, "I'll invest when the market goes back up and things look better." It was too late, though. The next year, it went up over 26%, followed by another 15% the year after. If you miss the train, you can try to hop back on the rail, but that growth is gone forever. You can't ever catch that first train again.

Perhaps the best example is in 2020 during COVID-19, just after this 20-year timeframe. Over just the first three months of 2020, the market was down around 20%. However, by the end of the year, not only did the market recover its losses, but it was up over 18%. If you had sold at the beginning of April, again citing that you would invest again once the market goes back up, when things look better, when this pandemic thing is under control, you would have missed the 38% swing. Your battery lost energy with the drop, and your solar panels were inside when the sun came back out in full force. I can't overstate this point: *that energy is lost forever.* Potentially, years and years worth of savings gone forever, all because the solar panels were in the shed.

What do all these examples have in common? Uncertainty. The stock market is what's called a leading indicator. That's a fancy way of saying it is trying to guess what is going to happen. When there is great uncertainty, it has no idea what is going to happen. This fear causes a selloff, pushing the market sharply down. The rhetoric always is, "But this time is different. This has never happened before." Well, of course, that is required for great uncertainty to exist. If something has happened before, then we know how it ended, right? There isn't uncertainty. Great uncertainty can only exist if something *hasn't* happened before—the internet looking like it was exploding, banks lending huge amounts of subprime debt, the first global pandemic in the modern era.

These are three substantial market downturns of over 20% within 20 years—how unusual! Actually, this is right on long-term averages. Every seven to eight years, this occurs, and as such, you should expect it to occur for you as well. Think about how old you are today. Think about how old you will be in 30 years. By the time you attain that age, you should expect to have had at least four more 20% market drops due to a new great uncertainty in the world.

Market corrections, a drop of 10%, are even more common, occurring once every 1–2 years. Think again of your future self 30 years down the road. By that time, you should also expect to have seen another 20 drops of 10% in the market.

I don't tell you all this to scare you; I tell it to you to prepare you. Just like you should expect 3 to 4 car accidents in your life, you should also expect these periodic market downturns. When the market is up, it is mentioned on the news. When the market is down, it is magnified on the news. It is up to you to pick which averages to focus on once your emotions become involved. The market being positive roughly 75% of the time in any one-year period, 85% of the time in any three-year period, 95% of the time in any 10-year period, and 100% of the time so far in any 15-year period are all equally valid averages as well.

Also, remember that if you are following the first step—being diversified—you won't be fully invested in just the S&P 500. In 2000, 2001, 2002, and 2008, this part of your portfolio may have gone down, but others may have gone up. Will you still have times when your accounts go down cumulatively? Absolutely. Do you have to enjoy it when it happens? Heck no! I certainly don't enjoy it one bit, but I do accept that they are going to occur periodically. Diversifying helps again to at least potentially smooth out those ups and downs while keeping us going in the right direction long term.

Developing a Planting and Harvesting Plan

(Sorry, I am almost done with my tree analogies here. At least you are not my wife having to hear me point out tree species on every walk . . .)

Some trees can be worth more. Some can grow more rapidly than others. Some are prone to more diseases. You need a plan for how conservative or aggressive your plantings will be. Part of this is how much uncertainty you are comfortable dealing with after learning about time and staying invested. The other part is determined by when you may need the tree to be harvested for use.

You may have noticed me referencing the 7% growth rate for my examples to this point in the book. You can see even at this rate, the numbers can grow to very substantial sums, roughly doubling every 10 years. The Rule of 72 states that if you divide your average return into 72, that is how long it takes for your account to double. If we assume 7%, that would be 72/7 = 10.28 years.

Long term (10+ years), a moderate portfolio may fall somewhere in this range, whereas a more aggressive or growth portfolio may be a bit higher, and a more conservative portfolio may be a bit lower. Using the same Rule of 72 above, a more aggressive 8% account would double in only 9 years (72/8), while a more conservative account would double in 12 years (72/6). While the aggressive portfolio should double the quickest, the ups and downs also become more extreme. There are more storms we need to be able to mentally weather and still leave our solar panels outside. The goal, therefore, is achieving as much consistency as possible, minding how much stormy weather we can tolerate, because this keeps us on track for where we want to go.

If your approach is too conservative, using only bank accounts to save, your financial battery will barely keep up with the rising costs of expenses. We once had someone come to us at retirement. They asked why their comparable coworkers, despite starting at the same time and saving virtually the same amount, had so much more money. When we reviewed their account, we found that they had invested 100% in a stable value fund—a code name for a money market. They had missed their opportunity for material compound growth; there was nothing we could do.

If your approach is too aggressive, selecting individual stocks, your financial battery can disappear all at once. We had another client who, despite our advice, invested 100% of their 401(k) in their company's stock. They argued the company was very strong, had been around forever, and there was no reason to believe it wouldn't continue indefinitely. They worked at Lehman Brothers. Their 401(k) of over $1,000,000 went down to $0. The chestnut blight got them, and once again, there was nothing we could do.

In the first example, they were too conservative. In the second example, they were what I would call irresponsibly aggressive. So what should you be? The answer is first to start with what you can emotionally handle. This sets your max for how aggressive you can be overall. Then, look at the timeline for when you need each account.

Let's say you are comfortable being aggressive, able to weather a more severe short-term storm, and not pull in your solar panels. If you have $100,000 in an IRA and you aren't going to retire for 20 years, this account can be invested aggressively. You will not need it for a long period of time. Based on the market downturn averages already discussed, it may go down more than 20% during three of those 20 years, but in this example, emotionally, you can handle it, and overall, an aggressive portfolio would give you the highest potential return for that period.

Notice here how it is time and not your age. If a 60-year-old has an IRA that they won't need for 20 years, that is the same as a 35-year-old who has an IRA they won't need for 20 years. We often say you can be aggressive when you are young, but really, what we are saying is you can be aggressive when you have sufficient time before you need the money.

Let's say, however, that you aren't comfortable being aggressive. Emotions always trump time. If a 20% drop in your portfolio, which should happen at least three times again during a 20-year span, is going to make you so uncomfortable that you can't sleep at night and pull all your money out of the market, taking those solar panels inside, it is virtually guaranteeing you miss out when the market comes back up. Here, an aggressive portfolio isn't appropriate for you, even though the time part of the equation is fitting as such, with you not needing the funds for 20 years. Instead, being moderately invested and only losing perhaps 10–15% when the market drops may be the most you can emotionally handle.

As a comparison, let's say you have a Joint Account, and you may need these funds in five years for college, a new home, or anything else. Here, because there is only a five-year window, a moderate account is likely the highest level that would be appropriate, even if you are comfortable being more aggressive in general.

As you progress in your life, you may accumulate more investment accounts, so you want to make sure the timing of when you may need them matches the appropriate level of aggressiveness while never crossing that line where you make yourself too uncomfortable in the short term to weather the temporary storms when they do occur.

Each account serves as its own cell and has its own purpose many times. Knowing when you expect to harvest each part of your forest determines how aggressively each part should be planted. I call this developing a Battery Harvesting Timeline, organizing each battery cell to ensure the timeline matches the appropriate level of investment risk.

A more involved example may look something like the one below. Again, this is one of the digital tools that can be found through the self-guided planning systems at TheFinancialPinwheel.com.

Battery Harvesting Timeline[IP]

John and Mary Smith			
Account	Timeline	Purpose	Risk Level
Joint	1 Year	New Roof	Lowest - Cash/CD
Joint	3 Years	Down Payment	Conservative
529 Plan	5 Years	Education	Moderate
John IRA	7 Years	1st Retirement Cell	Moderate
Mary IRA	9 Years	2nd Retirement Cell	Moderately Aggressive
Mary Roth IRA	15 Years	3rd Retirement Cell	Aggressive
John Roth IRA	20 Years	4th Retirement Cell	Aggressive

If John and Mary were to emotionally not be able to deal with any more than a moderate level of risk, however, then even the assets they don't need in 9+ years should likely also be moderately invested.

Following the DTSI rules will enable you to build a forest that can outlast the temporary storms, with solar panels growing to create your self-charging wind machine. It will start small; every forest only has little saplings at the beginning. As they grow, however, they become established, compounding their height over time, and you will see the forest emerge.

The Millionaire Exercise[IP]

My mentor came up with a version of this exercise to share with his daughters and their friends in high school. He would see their faces light up when realizing relatively small amounts could grow into substantial sums over time. Wealth was within their grasp. It was to try to inspire them through the education of savings and compound interest. I likewise share it with you, as it can be a fun exercise to see when you are currently on track to become a millionaire or, if you have already reached that mark, your track for the next million.

Find a number of periods calculator online (I have a few detailed below). Input your assumed interest rate (i), say, for example, 7%, if moderately invested, how much you currently have saved in investments (present value = PV), and how much you and your employer, if applicable, are saving each year so monthly savings x 12 (payment = PMT), and finally, set the future value to be 1,000,000 (FV).

For example, someone saving 1,000/mo with a 250/mo employer match and $100,000 already invested would be a millionaire in 20 years (7% growth). The inputs would look like this:

PV = 100,000
FV = 1,000,000
PMT = 15,000 ((1,000 + 250) x 12)
RATE (i) = 7

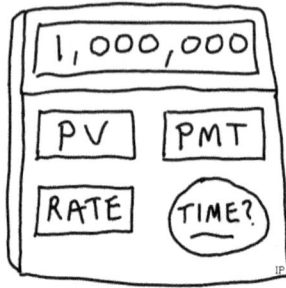

Online Calculators

1. https://captaincalculator.com/financial/time-value/number-of-periods-calculator/

2. https://www.calculator.net/finance-calculator.html (Click "N" for Periods Calculator - must input PV and PMT as negative numbers)

Part 3 Recap: A Self-Charging Wind Machine

1. Set Your DTSI Expectations

You don't want to be ditsy in life, but you want to be DTSI when it comes to investing.

Diversify: Spread out your funds everywhere, all the time.

- Target Date Funds – Managed fund that automatically becomes more conservative as it approaches that date.
- Allocation Fund – Managed fund that targets a specific level of risk.

Time: Historically speaking, consider the following time considerations.[14]

- 1 Day – Roughly a 50% chance the market will go up.
- 1 Year – Roughly a 75% chance the market will go up.
- 3 Years – Roughly an 85% chance the market will go up.
- 10 Years – Roughly a 95% chance the market will go up.
- 15 Years – To date, there has never been a 15-year period where the market was lower than it started.

Stay Invested: Keep your solar panels outside when storms occur, and they will.

- 10% Market Drop: Occur every 1–2 years on average.
- 20% Market Drop: Occur every 7–8 years on average.

2. Develop a Battery Harvesting Plan

Each account serves as its own cell and has its own purpose. This is how you determine how aggressive each battery cell should be, by when it is to be harvested.

John and Mary Smith			
Account	Timeline	Purpose	Risk Level
Joint	1 Year	New Roof	Lowest - Cash/CD
Joint	3 Years	Down Payment	Conservative
529 Plan	5 Years	Education	Moderate
John IRA	7 Years	1st Retirement Cell	Moderate
Mary IRA	9 Years	2nd Retirement Cell	Moderately Aggressive
Mary Roth IRA	15 Years	3rd Retirement Cell	Aggressive
John Roth IRA	20 Years	4th Retirement Cell	Aggressive

PART 4

Preparing for a Hurricane

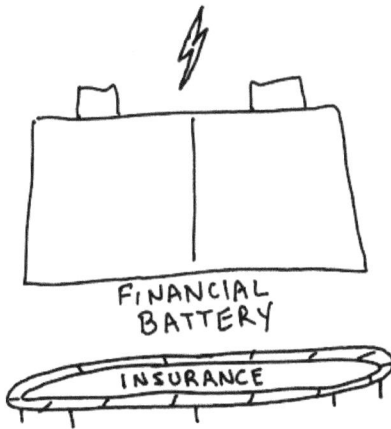

FINANCIAL
BATTERY

INSURANCE

Batten Down the Hatches

As the limerick goes, "In fourteen hundred ninety-two, Columbus sailed the ocean blue." The line left out, though, is, "In fourteen hundred ninety-five, Columbus sailed into a hurricane and barely survived."

Hurricanes used to strike without warning, devastating populations in areas such as the Caribbean and the Gulf of Mexico. We now have extensive monitoring systems and warnings to populations to try and prepare in advance. Even with these, it is never an exact science.

Exactly 500 years after Columbus' famous voyage, in 1992, Hurricane Andrew hit South Miami as a Category 5 hurricane. It quickly picked up speed and intensity, changing direction in the lead-up before smashing into South Miami. In 1992, there were warning systems, but the tracking error was not at the level it is today. Entire communities were destroyed, with Andrew's 165 mph winds leveling structures and literally ripping roofs off of houses, on its way to 27 billion in damages.

Despite the warnings, not everyone in the area was prepared. Some thought it would hit further north. Many had been through hurricanes before. If they had known how horrendous it was going to be, they would've taken extreme action. Every home would have been boarded up. Every resident that was able would have evacuated. We don't have perfect information, however, and so, just like with a real hurricane, we need to prepare in advance for what may occur.

Hurricane Ties

Hurricane Andrew would spark a huge push in advanced safety for home construction. From the actual architectural design to window strength, making the home more stable in the wake of extreme weather was paramount. One of the simplest and least expensive was hurricane ties, becoming a mandatory building element. These relatively small pieces of metal are hammered in to connect the roof to the home. The cost as of today is about $1 per tie. For just a few dollars, your home was significantly more protected.

The same is true for this wonderful pinwheel you are building. We have worked hard to have a good career, a steady income, and a flow of financial energy. We are saving every month into our financial batteries, which are becoming larger and larger as the solar panels compound their growth. We are right on the path for our perpetual pinwheel coming to fruition.

Then, a hurricane hits. It can take many forms: a spouse passes away, a car accident results in a disability, a fire destroys the home, financial energy stops coming in, and we have to start pulling excessively from our batteries. That path that just moments ago seemed so certain to be realized is now leveled, a smashed-up pinwheel in the wake of the hurricane.

These are all things that we know can happen but are easier just not to think about. There is no way around the fact that this part just isn't fun. Creating something, like a perpetual pinwheel, is exciting. We are making something new, something we can see, for goals we want to imagine. If we do not protect it, though, it is like not heeding the warning of a real coming hurricane. This is your warning to take action, and as you'll see, just like the hurricane ties, it can be surprisingly easy to install.

Insuring for the Catastrophic

When you buy a dishwasher, a cell phone, or any other relatively basic consumer staple, they almost always offer you a warranty to go along with it. If this device breaks, you will want the warranty, they say, and look how affordable it is! If you want to buy the warranty for these items, you can. If you are like most consumers, the majority of the time, you pass on the insurance. If your dishwasher breaks, it's not fun, but it is also not the end of the world. You will be able to get it fixed or buy a new one without your pinwheel collapsing. The loss is not catastrophic.

On the other hand, if someone dies, becomes disabled, wrecks their car, is sued, or has their house burned down, that is a catastrophic loss. These are events, if unprotected, that can lead to devastation and, as such, need to be insured against.

The 5 Empty Boats[IP]

A man is enjoying himself on a river at dusk. He sees another boat coming down the river toward him. At first, it seems so nice to him that another boat is enjoying the river on a calm summer evening. Then, he realizes the boat is directed to come right toward him. He begins to voice his concern. "Hey, watch out!" It stays the course, though, and is now picking up speed. He tries again, this time much sterner than the first. "Hey, get out of the way! We'll crash if you don't move," but still nothing. It comes faster and faster still. By this time, he is standing in his boat, screaming and shaking his fists. "What are you insane?!" Finally, the boat smashes right into him. As he recovers from the shock, he stands up, full of fury, only to look inside, where he sees that it's an empty boat. As he stood in disbelief, another boat, also from down the river, came alongside him.

"Did you see that?" the furious man asked the newcomer.

"Yes," the newcomer replied. "The boat went past me first on its way towards you."

"You were lucky," the furious man replied. "It missed you. I wasn't so lucky."

"Well," said the newcomer, "I saw that it might hit me, so I moved out of the way."

In life, there are lots and lots of empty boats on our river. We would like to think that everything is as it should be, that all boats have responsible captains, and everything is in control. We know it doesn't work that way, though.

Whether it be a stray boat or a hurricane, we need to protect our Financial Pinwheel we have now created. There are five main empty boats we need to protect our pinwheel against.

I cover all five of these boats in greater detail found through the self-guided planning systems at TheFinancial-Pinwheel.com.

Boat 1: Life Insurance

Most people are familiar with life insurance. If you pass away, you obviously cannot earn income or produce financial energy for the pinwheel to spin. Life Insurance is like a giant financial battery that will be given to your family if you pass away. Instead of slowly building up your financial battery on your own, it is given to you now, all at once.

This battery through life insurance needs to be large enough, though, to replicate everything your family may need in the long term.

For example, if you bring home $5,000/mo to the family and are on track with your savings to attain a perpetual pinwheel in 10 years, then the amount you need today is $5,000 x 12 months x 10 years = $600,000. Notice that you do not need the insurance forever; you need the insurance until you attain a perpetual pinwheel. At that point, even if you were to pass, the perpetual pinwheel would be powered the same way for your spouse.

This is the first way to calculate your life insurance needs based on the retirement gap. The second way to calculate is based on a 5% rule. Here, you are dividing your take-home pay by 5% instead.

Taking the same example above, you would reach $1,200,000 ($5,000 x 12 months / 5%). Whichever method comes out *lower* is the one you can use. The years-to-retirement gap tends to make more sense for those closer to retirement. The 5% Rule Method[IP] tends to make more sense for younger individuals.

For example, if we calculated the same two methods for someone 30 years from retirement, you can see how this changes the result. The years to retirement method would be much larger, at $1,800,000 ($5,000 x 12 months x 30 years), whereas the 5% rule stays the same at $1,200,000. What happens in the 5% rule version is that assuming the insurance funds are invested, they are able to generate enough return to make up for the lower starting value over a longer period of time.

Initially, either option may seem like an unreasonably large amount. However, remember: this needs to replace your entire earnings potential for up to the next 30 years. That is a really big number to cover. Luckily, for healthy individuals, it can also be like a hurricane tie—very reasonably affordable.

There are two general ways to obtain life insurance: individually or through your employer. If you obtain it through your employer, it is very simple, with the premiums deducted from your paycheck. If you are not in good health, this may be your only affordable option, as employer life insurance works on a group basis, meaning your individual health situation is not evaluated prior to providing at least up to a certain amount of coverage. The big disadvantage here is that your insurance cannot easily travel with you. If you lose or change jobs, then the insurance goes away too. There is a gap in coverage, and the new plan may not be sufficient for your needs.

This is why if you can afford to do so, which, if you are in good health, should be true, I recommend having individual life insurance policies. Here, you can choose between term, universal, and whole-life options. Outside of special circumstances, I would almost always recommend term insurance, as you are only paying for the insurance you need, not paying the insurance company above the cost of insurance to build up savings with them as well. In my opinion, these savings are much better put to use in your investments instead.

For example, a 20-year term policy for a 40-year-old male at that $1.25M level would come out to around just $60/mo for a preferred rated individual. A whole life policy, in contrast, might be 10–15x more expensive. Even if you can afford the $600/mo, I would rather see the $60/mo go towards your insurance and the remaining $540 go towards an employer match, Roth IRA, or any other personal investment account. You have flexibility and choice, and pulling out all the savings does not result in loan payments or loss of the insurance you need as with a whole life policy.

When in doubt, lean on the high side for coverage. Your income will increase over time, so having a bit of a buffer built in is never a bad idea. A widow has never said they wished their spouse had less in life insurance. Because it can be so affordable, it should not be cost-prohibitive either to do so. If that $1.25M policy was bumped to $1.5M, it might be just an additional $10/mo.

Boat 2: Disability Insurance

While life insurance is more known and discussed, disability insurance is actually statistically more important to have. You are around 3x more likely to have a disability versus a death during your working years. Furthermore, unlike death, you not only have no income, but you also continue to have basic living expenses that need to be met. You will probably even have more expenses overall with increasing medical outlays depending on the injury, resulting in a bigger pinwheel and less financial energy.

Short-term disability generally covers the first 90–180 days, while long-term disability is beyond that. Your state may cover short-term up to a certain level, so it is a good place to start with reviewing. Short-term is not catastrophic, as your Emergency Fund, as we already discussed, should be able to cover you if needed. Long-term disability is the greater focus here, covering you generally after 90–180 days to age 65.

As with life insurance, disability insurance can be purchased individually or through your employer. Employer insurance, however, is significantly more affordable, with most employers in the matching world covering the first 50% and an affordable buy-up option to 60%. For a very modest price, buying up and getting additional coverage is the right approach. An extra 10% of your income long-term, if disabled, will be infinitely appreciated.

Any benefit received that the employer pays for comes to you as taxable income. Any benefit received in which you paid the premium comes to you tax-free. Pay attention to the length of coverage, elimination period (waiting period—90/180 days), and maximum monthly benefit to ensure adequate coverage.

If your employer does not provide, you are self-employed, or you are financially flexible enough to purchase individually, a self-funded policy can provide a more lasting and comprehensive level of protection. If you purchase individually, changing employers has no effect. The policy will continue as long as you pay your premiums. It can also be tailored to cover your specific occupation and skill set, so if, for example, you are a surgeon and hurt your eye, you may not be able to perform surgery. If your individual policy is a true-own occupation, you would still qualify for benefits even though you can still perform other jobs such as teaching or otherwise. Disability policies come with a myriad of options, and different carriers can specialize in different professions, so having a thorough agent here is especially important.

Social security can also provide disability coverage, but it can be difficult to qualify for, will require ongoing proof to stay active, and likely won't cover your current income level. Relying on social security disability alone is not a wise approach.

Single-income households or those with income significantly tied to one spouse are especially at risk, with disability meaning up to 100% of income disappearing.

Boat 3: Property and Casualty (Home, Auto, and Umbrella)

Most everyone has home and auto insurance, quite simply because it is required to obtain a mortgage or purchase a car. Many, though, look for the cheapest coverage, which can mean the most stripped down and limited. You should be familiar with what your policy offers, deductibles, and medical claims as starters. Coverage inside and outside your home differs; for example, the sewer line between your home and the street may not be covered. A condo or multifamily property can create other wrinkles. Here again, a thorough agent can be very helpful. A few hundred more a year may be worth significantly better protection.

One of the biggest concerns in our current world is lawsuits, especially depending on the state. New Jersey, for example, where I reside, is certainly prone to such occurrences, with minor fender benders turning into high six-figure lawsuits. A base-level policy may have $300,000 in liability (lawsuit) protection for a car accident or injury on your property. An umbrella policy, as it is known, because it covers your auto and your home insurance, can add another million or more to your liability protection. It generally costs just a few hundred per year to do so, making it again a very cost-effective measure for catastrophic protection of your pinwheel.

Boat 4: Long-Term Care Insurance

This insurance provides funding in the case of elder care expenses down the road. One of the most common misconceptions is that Medicare covers long-term care expenses. It does not. Outside of temporary facility coverage in a rehab scenario, Medicare will not provide you with long-term care coverage. It is on you. Medicaid only steps in if you have spent virtually all your assets.

These expenses quickly reach tens of thousands and easily exceed over one hundred thousand a year based on location and level of care. For the insurance to be affordable at all, obtaining it prior to age 55 is almost required. Because medicine is able to keep people alive much longer than before but not necessarily in a state of living that is self-dependent, this is one of the most expensive insurances. It was also so grossly mispriced early in its development that many carriers pulled out altogether, while others have had to implement rate increases to keep benefit pools intact.

Planning for these needs is most important for couples, as the majority do not have the funds available to afford an additional $100,000 or more per year. It can leave the surviving spouse destitute. Here, a plan needs to be put in place, whether through long-term care insurance, self-funding, insurance products with long-term care benefit riders, or some hybrid approach.

Self-funding is for individuals who have in excess of their retirement income needs and can simply set aside a pool of, say, $300,000 to fund any expenses down the road. The advantage here is that there are no premiums, and if you never need the care, all these assets are preserved. The disadvantage is that you are not leveraging an insurance carrier to help cover a cost if it does arise.

Insurance products can include life insurance riders or annuity riders. Here, you pay an additional fee to the insurance company to have funding in the case of these needs. The advantage is leverage. The disadvantage is you pay a fee for a benefit you may never utilize.

If none of these are plausible options for you, then leveraging your home equity could be an emergency fallback plan as well. Downsizing, a new mortgage or equity loan, or even a reverse mortgage can access that equity in an emergency scenario such as long-term care. These can be expensive and cause additional debt, so careful consideration is needed prior to enacting.

There needs to be some plan, though. Without any means of addressing this, you will need to spend down virtually all of your assets prior to Medicaid, not Medicare, kicking in. Medicaid is to help those with no financial means, so you need to have essentially no assets before it will assist. It also will not cover any facility you want, so the care may not be what you ideally desire. Medicaid is run at the state level, so there can be some intricacies in the exact rules depending on where you live, and it is wise to review in advance.

Boat 5: Legal Documents (Will/POA/Living Will/Medical Directive/ Trusts)

The last empty boat is the most unpredictable of all. The other boats cover specific scenarios: death, disability, accident, long term care. This empty boat can take many different forms and is more about providing you with flexibility and the right individual emergency powers to handle the unexpected.

Wills

A will is the most basic and familiar. It is more than just saying who gets your stuff, though. If you have young children, it says who you would want to raise them. It can also say if a separate individual from the child's guardian is to handle the financial responsibilities. Think about what friend or family member you would want to raise your children and handle their money. Now think about what friend or family member would likely best be able to *convince a judge* they should raise your children and handle their money. Are they the same person? Without your direction, the latter could likely end up with the responsibility.

A will only covers assets that pass through it via a process called probate. This is the courts being involved in your assets passing to your heirs. Not every asset goes through probate, though. Most of your assets may not. Retirement accounts, life insurance, and annuities, for example, do not pass through the will and subsequently probate. They almost always have direct beneficiaries listed, and for good reason—it is the quickest and most tax-efficient way for them to receive the assets. While you can list your estate as the beneficiary, enabling the details of your will to carry forth for distribution, it causes immediate taxation on all retirement and annuity assets. This can cause large amounts of additional and unnecessary taxation.

When you appoint an executor (male) or executrix (female), this is simply the person who has to carry out the details of the will and settle the estate. It is not a fun or easy task. Being an executor is not on my list of things to do in life. This person should be capable, reliable, and preferably detail-oriented. We have had estates take multiple years to fully distribute due to the wrong individual being in control. Having multiple individuals in this role for equality's sake is also not recommended. If you have two children, you may have the urge to appoint them both so no one feels left out. This only complicates things, with now two people needing to authorize and agree on every decision legally.

Trusts

Trusts are one of the items I am asked about quite frequently, as you hear about them regularly from well-to-do friends and in movies. They are associated with wealthy people. Trusts are not good or bad; however, they are simply tools if there is a specific problem to solve. If there is not a specific problem to solve, they can just complicate things unnecessarily.

An example problem could be a child with a disability, as they should not inherit assets directly. Here, they should have a special needs trust. A child with substance abuse would be another example. A trust to limit distributions to gainful means for that child. A family home is yet another example where the goal is to keep it in the family for generations. It being in a trust can share ownership and protect the generational legacy. Notice that every scenario has a specific problem it is trying to solve: special needs, addiction, and family legacy. They are not created simply for the sake of creation. It is a separate legal entity with a tax ID, a trustee administering, and a requirement to file taxes just like you or me. I've had clients with trusts where I asked about the benefit of the trust and what it was helping to accomplish that couldn't have been accomplished without it. Many times, I have been answered with blank faces.

One of the most common trusts can be one for your beneficiaries when you pass, especially if they are a minor, referred to as a trust under the will (T/U/W). The advantage here is that no trust needs to be created or administered now. It is created when you pass, with the will dictating its exact rules and formation. Most investment accounts will allow this to be listed as a beneficiary, but insurance companies are not always willing to do so.

So again, start with what problem you want to solve, and then see if the tool that is a trust could help in solving it. Don't start with wanting a trust and seeing how to fit one in.

Power of Attorney (POA)

This document is usually formed in conjunction with a will and the living will with a medical directive detailed immediately below. Here, you are giving another individual power to act on your behalf, either immediately now or under certain circumstances. The circumstance usually is if you are incapacitated in some way.

This can be crucially important, as a financial institution cannot take direction from someone not listed on the account as an owner. If all your household investments are in your spouse's IRA, only they can withdraw money from it, not you, even if it is an emergency. Saying you really need it doesn't matter. The power of attorney gives you this flexibility.

Imagine something terrible happening to someone you love. You are emotionally a wreck. Is going to the courts to try and obtain a power of attorney during a crisis something you want to do? We have had this happen to clients with older parents who needed to get this necessary authority during times of crisis.

It is important to mention that this authority stops once the individual passes away. It is power in life, not death. Once someone passes, it is the executor or executrix who now steps into authority.

Like the will, it is generally best to appoint this as a one-individual at a time authority, not a shared authority. Two children with equal power and different ideas is a recipe for conflict and inefficiency on your behalf. Determining who legally makes the decision instead of them removes any potential issues. You also do not have to have the same individual for every document. One child can serve, for example, in one role, and a separate child can serve in another.

Living Will with a Medical Directive

This is the last of the major legal documents determining who you want to be making medical decisions on your behalf if you cannot. It would also include what your medical desires may be (do-not-resuscitate or DNR order)—although you may commonly have heard people refer to it less eloquently as "pulling the plug."

As with the will and POA, having one individual serve in this capacity avoids any conflicts with decision-making.

Part 4 Recap: Preparing for a Hurricane

1. Boat 1: Life Insurance

If you pass away, you obviously cannot earn income and cannot produce financial energy for the pinwheel to spin. Life Insurance is like a giant financial battery that will be given to your family if you pass away. Instead of slowly building up your financial battery on your own, it is given to you now, all at once.

Needs Calculations (Use Lower)

- Method 1: Years to Retirement - Annual Take Home Pay x Years Until Retirement
- Method 2: 5% Rule - Annual Take Home Pay / 5%

2. Boat 2: Disability Insurance

You are around 3x more likely to have a disability versus a death during your working years. Furthermore, unlike death, you not only have no income, but you also continue to have basic living expenses that need to be met. You will probably even have more expenses overall with increasing medical outlays depending on the injury, resulting in a bigger pinwheel and less financial energy.

Disability Types

- Short-Term Disability (STD): Usually 30–180 days
- Long-Term Disability (LTD): Usually from 90–180 days to age 65

3. Boat 3: Property and Casualty (Home, Auto, and Umbrella)

Look to obtain proper coverage, not the cheapest coverage. Umbrella policies can provide significantly more protection for liability (lawsuit) protection—$1M or more—at just a few hundred per year.

4. Boat 4: Long-Term Care Insurance

This insurance provides funding in the case of elder care expenses down the road. One of the most common misconceptions is that Medicare covers long-term care expenses. It does not. Medicaid only steps in if you have spent virtually all your assets.

LTC Approaches

Long-term care insurance	Potential high level of coverage, but if no claims needed, expensive premiums are lost
Self-Funding pool	No premiums and full asset control, but no insurer to leverage to share costs if needed
Hybrid insurance (life/annuity)	Insurer leveraged coverage, but if unused, additional fees for coverage are lost
Home Equity	Likely an emergency option, as would require a new mortgage or selling home

5. Boat 5: Legal Documents

The last empty boat is the most unpredictable of all. The other boats cover specific scenarios: death, disability, accident, and long-term care. This empty boat can take many different forms and is more about providing you with flexibility and the right individual emergency powers to handle the unexpected.

Documents to Obtain

- Will – Who your assets transfer to if you pass
- Power of Attorney (POA) – Who can take legal action on your behalf while living
- Living Will/Medical Directive – Medical desires and agent if you aren't capable
- Trust – Likely only applicable if you need to plan for a special situation

> If you want more assistance on any of the items discussed in Part 4, look at TheFinancialPinwheel.com for more resources to help.

The Pinwheel Action Plan^{IP}

The Holiday Roast

A little girl was at her family's holiday party. She danced about, spinning to see how far her fancy dress would twirl around as she did. Finishing a twirl, she glanced into the kitchen as adults were preparing the meal to come. She noticed her mother seasoning a roast with a variety of spices before finally cutting off the ends and placing it in a pan. The girl found this quite odd.

"Mom," she asked with a tilt of her head, the curls of her hair falling to one side behind her, "why do you cut the ends off before you put it in the pan?"

Her mom gazed with a smile of admiration for her curiosity and then looked at the roast, readying her reply before realizing she didn't really have one. "I'm actually not sure, dear. This is the way my mother always prepared it."

As it was a family event, the grandmother of the girl was present as well. Going up with her mother, the little girl asked again, "Grandma, why do you cut the ends off the roast before you put it in the pan?"

The grandmother chuckled and looked at the mother before realizing there wasn't an answer between them. "I don't know, Honey," she replied. "That is the way my mother always did it."

Fortunately, they were lucky enough that the girl's great-grandmother was still alive and present. The girl, her mother, and her grandmother all made their way over to her, with the girl repeating the same question as before: "Great grandmother, why do you cut the ends off the roast before you put it in the pan?"

The old woman looked up at the girl and smiled. After a moment, she slowly replied, "Well, that is an easy one, my dear." The girl, mother, and grandmother all leaned in with anticipation. The great-grandmother continued, "That was the only way I could fit it into my oven."

This book starts with how we can make decisions in one of two ways. The first is making a decision based on what we have already learned up to this point in time. The second is by learning something new. You now have learned something new. You can continue doing things in the same way you are accustomed to for whatever reasons seemed to previously make sense, cutting off the ends of the roast. Your other option, though, and I will say the better option, is to make new decisions based on what you have now learned.

To try and assist, this section includes how to put these various parts in motion. How to develop your Pinwheel Action Plan.

How or Who

If Usain Bolt had prepared poorly and run a terrible race, he would likely still have won. He is arguably the best track athlete of all time. He was starting from such a high place of possibility that even if he got a slow start or pulled up at the end, he would probably be fine.

If he wanted to do the best he could, though, if he wanted to finish at the top end of his possibility, he needed to train hard and have help. He wouldn't use the free training app on Apple Play; he would get the best trainers he could find.

Someone in the Pension Arena will probably be fine if they simply save 5–10% of their income and take the necessary protection steps. They may not hit the top of their possibility, but they should finish the race without a problem.

Someone in the Matching or Entrepreneurial Arenas who saves 30% of their income will also probably be fine. Even if they don't follow every investment step to maximize their possibility, they are saving such a significant amount, keeping their pinwheel to such a manageable size, that they again should finish the race without a problem.

The thing is, most people aren't in this space; most people need to make choices to maximize their possibility to be fine. Still, others, maybe you, want to be more than fine regardless. They want to maximize their possibility so they can enjoy life as much as possible. More vacations, early retirement, pay for education, and every other goal they imagine.

You either have to learn how, with this book and the self-guided tools at TheFinancialPinwheel.com, or you need to find a who to guide you who already knows.

How – The Self-Guided Pinwheel Action Plan

This book and the resources I have developed, in conjunction with it both in this chapter and via the self-guided courses at TheFinancialPinwheel.com, are geared toward those who want to know how. You are reading this book most likely because you want help doing it on your own. If you decide you may not want to do it on your own after reading, the subsequent "who" section can assist.

For those who want a self-guided option, that is great; any steps you can take forward are fantastic. The framework I have developed speaks specifically to getting you there. I have developed two resources to implement. The first is a

9-step guide with checklists to mark off as you go, which is listed below.

The other resource is a much more interactive online resource that you can find at TheFinancialPinwheel.com. This includes a self-guided Pinwheel Playbook for your situation. It will guide you to the customized playbook that is most fitting for you. Here, you will have access to not only digital checklists but also videos from me that personally walk you through the concepts. There are even calculation sheets, so you don't have to do any of the math on your own (hooray!), as well as short confirmation exercises at the end of each chapter to help solidify your understanding. It is priced to be affordable for absolutely everyone.

Try one, try both—whatever works for you is the best approach to take. When going through the 9-step guide provided below, I encourage you to refer back to the recaps for each of the four parts as needed to help refresh your memory. Believe it or not, that is why I included recaps for each!

Step 1 – Your Current Pinwheel

We start at the beginning. How big is this pinwheel you want to spin? First, we want to know your Employment Arena so you know what path you have chosen when it comes to pinwheel size and required savings.

- ❑ My Employment Arena is _____
- ❑ My Spouse's Employment Arena is _____
- ❑ Monthly Pinwheel Size Calculation
  - Total Household Take Home Pay: _____
  - Total Savings after Take Home Pay: _____
  - **= Financial Pinwheel Size** _____

Remember that here, you are only focusing on savings from your take-home pay. Any work plan contributions are not relevant. A 401(k) contribution, for example, comes out before your take-home pay is received. It would not be included.

Anything you receive in your pocket, your take-home pay, is either saved or spent. Those are the only two options. It only qualifies as savings if you don't touch it at all. Money you save into your Roth IRA or Joint Investment Account every month counts as savings. Money you put into a savings account and then use for your annual vacation does not.

Step 2 – Your Current Financial Battery

While Step 1 deals with the size of your pinwheel, Step 2 will help you organize how your financial battery is situated. How much have you already saved? How much do you continue to save every month? For your pinwheel in Step 1 to someday spin perpetually, you need to build up your financial batteries. Can you put any more financial energy away toward yourself?

Check off each that is true. Those not checked off are the ones that need to be worked on.

Protection Cell (Short-Term)

- ❑ My Emergency Fund Cell = $_____
  (2–6 months of pinwheel needs)
- ❑ My savings for short-term goals = $_____
  (goals < 2 years) in savings, money market, or CDs

Flexibility Cell (Intermediate-Term)

❑ I have a Joint or Individual investment account

Monthly Contribution = $_____

Flexibility Cell Value = $_____

Growth Cell (Long Term)

❑ Taking advantage of my employer match (free money!)

❑ Spouse taking advantage of their employer match (free money!)

❑ Utilizing a Roth 401k or Roth IRA, if eligible (tax-free growth)

Monthly Contribution = $_____

Roth Growth Cell = $_____

❑ Utilizing a Traditional 401k or IRA (tax-deductible contributions)

Monthly Contribution = $_____

Non-Roth Growth Cell = $_____

Step 3 – Your Current Savings %

Using the savings information gathered in Step 2, calculate what percent you are currently saving. Remember, those who are in the Pension Arena require a lower savings rate (5–10%) than those in the Matching (15–30%) or Entrepreneurial (15–35%) Arenas. These, on average, generally target at least a 20% savings rate unless they are starting early (15%) or late (25–35%).

Savings Rate Exercise

	Individual	Spouse (if applicable)	
Monthly Savings			(ex: 200 Joint + 800 401k = 1k/mo)
Gross Income			(ex: 12,500/mo)
Percent Saved			(ex: 1,000 / 12,500 = 8%)
Employer Match			(ex: 3%)
Saving Rate %			(ex: 8% + 3% = 11%)
Household Savings			(ex: 1,000 + 700)
Household Match $			(ex: 3% x 12.5k + 5% x 10,000)
Household Total			(ex: 1,700 + 875)
Household Gross Inc.			(ex: 12,500 + 10,000)
Household Savings %			(ex: 2,575 / 22,500)

Step 4 – Pinwheel Multiplier: Your Current Financial Battery

This exercise is most helpful if you are in the Matching or Entrepreneurial Arena. (The Pension Arena is pretty straightforward: a 5–10% savings rate for most of your working career is likely sufficient.)

If you and your spouse are both in the Matching and/ or Entrepreneurial Arenas, you can complete this exercise cumulatively. If one spouse is in the Pension Arena, you can exclude their portion and focus only on the income from the other spouse.

Pinwheel Multiplier Exercise

| | Pinwheel Multiplier | |
Age	Standard	High Income (500k)
30	1.50	2.25
35	2.00	3.00
40	3.50	5.25
45	5.00	7.50
50	6.50	9.75
55	8.00	12.00
60	10.00	15.00
65	12.50	18.75

Annual Pinwheel		Pinwheel Multiplier	Target Investments
	X		

Step 5 - Battery Supercharging Opportunities

If your financial batteries are not exactly where you'd like them right now, are there any upcoming supercharging opportunities you may be able to leverage?

Battery Supercharging Opportunities

- ❏ I have a car loan expense ending = $_____
  - ❏ I will save once available
- ❏ I have daycare expenses ending = $_____
  - ❏ I will save once available
- ❏ I receive a bonus every year = $_____
  - ❏ I will save a portion = %_____
- ❏ I receive a tax refund every year = $_____
  - ❏ I will save a portion = %_____
- ❏ I will receive an inheritance = $_____
  - ❏ I will save once available
- ❏ I reviewed my mortgage for possible refinance opportunities

Step 6 – DTSI

You now know the size of your financial batteries. Are you following the DTSI rules to make the most of them? Your solar panels need to be arranged appropriately and pointed at the sun. This allows the batteries to grow while you are working and self-charge in retirement, allowing the perpetual pinwheel to last forever. Build that forest.

Diversification

- ❏ All work plans are utilizing target date fund investments
- ❏ All non-work investments are utilizing allocation funds

- ❏ Battery cells are invested accordingly for timeline and risk
- ❏ Short-term cells are more conservative
- ❏ Intermediate-term cells are appropriate for the time needed
- ❏ Long-term cells are as aggressive as is comfortable

Time Behavior

20% Market Drops, I expect to see

- ❏ Years until my retirement   _____
- ❏ Years until retirement divided by 7   _____
- ❏ I expect to see this many 20% market declines before I retire

10% Market Drops, I expect to see

- ❏ Years until my retirement
- ❏ Years until retirement divided by 1.5 _____
- ❏ I expect to see this many 10% market declines before I retire

Staying Investing (S&P 500)

- ❏ I acknowledge any one day has had a roughly 50% chance of being positive
- ❏ I acknowledge any one year has had a roughly 75% chance of being positive
- ❏ I acknowledge any three years has had a roughly 85% chance of being positive

❏ I acknowledge any ten years has had a roughly 95% chance of being positive

❏ I acknowledge any 15 years has always been positive to date

Required disclosure: Past performance is no guarantee of future results.

Step 7 – Battery Harvesting Timeline

Organize your accounts into the table below so you can see when you will need each, making sure the longer the time horizon, the more aggressive each account becomes. Remember to never exceed the maximum level of aggressiveness you can emotionally handle, even if it may be appropriate from a time horizon perspective.

Battery Harvesting Timeline[IP]			
Account	Timeline	Purpose	Risk Level

Step 8 – Protecting Against the 5 Empty Boats

You may now have all your accounts organized and be on a great savings track. If you are not protecting your financial batteries from possible catastrophic scenarios, though, that could all go to waste. This is the least fun step. Do it anyway.

1. Life Insurance

- ❑ I have term life insurance outside my employer
- ❑ My spouse has term life insurance outside their employer
- ❑ My insurance term covers my family from now until retirement
- ❑ I have calculated my insurance need (use smaller number)

    Method 1: Years to Retirement
    - ❑ A. My annual take-home pay _____
    - ❑ B. Years until retirement _____
    - ❑ C. My insurance need (A x B) _____

    Method 2: 5% Rule
    - ❑ A. My annual take-home pay _____
    - ❑ B. My insurance need (A / 5%)_____

2. Disability Insurance

- ❑ I have short-term disability coverage (state and/or individual policy)
- ❑ My spouse has short-term disability coverage (state and/or individual policy)

❑ I have long-term disability coverage (60% coverage is ideal)
❑ My spouse has long-term disability coverage (60% coverage is ideal)

3. Property and Casualty Insurance (Home, Car, Umbrella)

❑ I have reviewed my homeowner's insurance to ensure adequate coverage
❑ I have reviewed my auto insurance to ensure adequate coverage
❑ I have obtained an umbrella policy to provide additional liability protection

4. Long-Term Care Insurance

❑ I acknowledge Medicare does not provide long-term care protection
❑ Looking into long-term care insurance prior to age 55 is likely necessary
❑ I have a plan to cover my long-term care needs

1. Long-term care insurance	Potential high level of coverage, but if no claims are needed, expensive premiums are lost
2. Self-funding pool	No premiums and full asset control, but no insurer to leverage to share costs if needed

3. Hybrid insurance (life/annuity)   Insurer leveraged coverage, but if unused, additional fees for coverage are lost

4. Home Equity   Likely an emergency option, as it would require a new mortgage or selling home

5. Legal Documents

- ❑ I have an up-to-date will
- ❑ I have an up-to-date power of attorney
- ❑ I have an up-to-date living will with medical directive
- ❑ I have established trusts *only if* there are special planning considerations

Step 9 – Annual Pinwheel Review

Congratulations! You have organized your Financial Pinwheel and have an action plan now to show for it! Seeing all those boxes checked off should give you confidence that you have those items under control, as well as provide you with a list of items still needing attention to bring you the rest of the way.

The pinwheel is always in motion, though. It needs to be reviewed periodically to ensure it continues on a path to become perpetual. For example, as your income changes, the size of your pinwheel changes with it. At least a portion of this financial energy needs to be directed back toward your financial batteries., You should review your Financial Pinwheel annually or sooner if material changes occur.

- Annual Pinwheel Review

  ❏ Recalculate Pinwheel Size
  ❏ Review your Financial Batteries and growth
  ❏ Recalculate your Savings Rate
  ❏ Recalculate target Financial Battery size
  ❏ Identify any new Battery Supercharging opportunities
  ❏ Remind yourself to stay DTSI
  ❏ Review battery harvesting timeline and risk tolerances
  ❏ Review your protection coverages

Who – Finding the Right Guide

I sincerely hope that between this book, the 9-step action plan guide, and the online interactive resources through TheFinancialPinwheel.com, you have enough resources to feel organized and confident in your finances.

If you feel overwhelmed, have an overly complex situation that requires more detailed planning, or simply realize this isn't what you want to spend your time doing, then finding the right "who" is paramount. Whether from you or someone else, your financial pinwheel needs planning and attention.

Here are some things to look for when finding the right Financial Pinwheel Professional.

1. **Fiduciary Status:** This means they legally must put your interests ahead of their own. Make sure to clarify which aspects of their advice fall under this fiduciary requirement.

2. **Planning Focus:** If they spend the majority of the time speaking about investments, they are not the right fit. Investments are just a tool, and you are not at Home Depot. You want someone who focuses primarily on planning. A certified financial planner, CFP®, can be a good start but doesn't always guarantee they are planning-focused either, unfortunately.

3. **Phenomenal Questions:** I tell my advisors they need to be phenomenal question-askers. They need to understand where you are now, where you are going, and what concerns you have in getting there. They can't do that by talking; they need to do that by listening. They should be asking you questions you didn't even think about in order to understand your pinwheel completely.

4. **Connection and Trust:** This individual is to help give you the confidence and clarity about your pinwheel so that you can focus just on enjoying life. You should like them, have a connection with them, and feel that you can trust them fully.

5. **Fees for Service:** This is last for good reason. You don't want the cheapest adviser. You want the best adviser. Know what you are paying for, but focus on how much clarity and confidence their planning is providing in building your eventual perpetual pinwheel. It needs to spin forever.

My Ongoing Service to You

Have you ever noticed that no matter how many pages a book contains, there always seems to be enough room to tell you exactly what the book is about on the back cover? If a book really needed 500 pages, how could it be summarized in exactly the same space as a 150-page book?

I wanted this book to be simple. Simple is different than easy, mind you. If I ask where the nearest restaurant is, and they answer down at the end of this road, that may be simple. It is down the end of the road I am already on. No problem, one direction.

However, if that road is five miles long and I'm walking, it is not easy. Everything in this book is designed to be simple. You can do it. Everything, though, is not necessarily easy. Finances are not intrinsically fun. No number of analogies and adapted fables will change that. You probably won't really want to take the time to do many of the steps.

They are important, though, so I encourage you to take enough steps to understand your pinwheel, the path you are on towards making it perpetual, and how to protect it along the way.

Signing up for your own specialized Pinwheel Playbook at TheFinancialPinwheel.com is the single most impactful step you can take.

If I were to offer to come out to your home and personally walk you through all these concepts, you would probably welcome the additional assistance. While I like a good challenge, that is obviously not something I can do.

Your self-guided Pinwheel Playbook is the next best thing. Here, we provide you with regular check-ins, updates, and encouragement to give enough focus so that your perpetual pinwheel becomes a reality. Leverage us and our resources.

Thank you for exploring the Financial Pinwheel with me. Keep on spinning.

THE FINANCIAL PINWHEEL[IP]

BUILDING YOUR PERPETUAL FINANCIAL ENERGY MACHINE

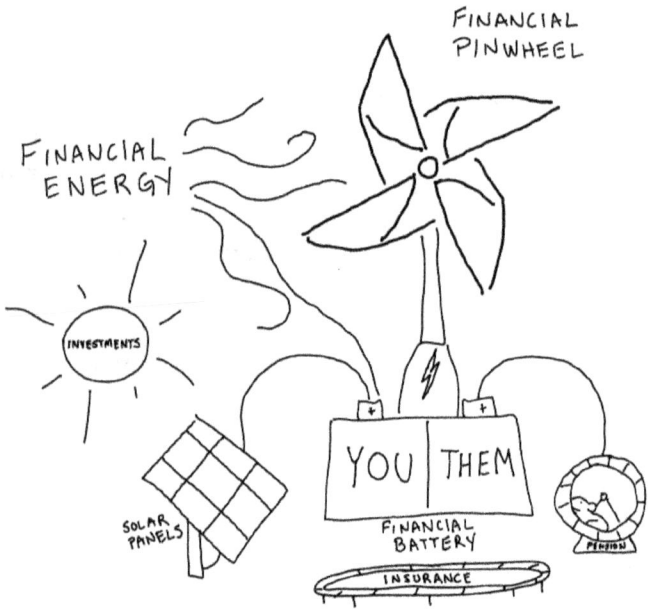

Endnotes

1   Pablo S. Torre, "How (and Why) Athletes Go Broke - Sports Illustrated Vault," SI.com, March 23, 2009, https://vault.si.com/vault/2009/03/23/how-and-why-athletes-go-broke.

2   Callum Jones, "How Mike Tyson Made a Fortune, Went Bankrupt and Then Rebuilt It All Again," UNILAD, July 5, 2023, https://www.unilad.com/celebrity/how-mike-tyson-went-bankrupt-and-rebuilt-220508-20230705.

3   Lisette Hilton, "Skating Was Passion, Therapy for Hamill," ESPN, accessed September 1, 2024, https://www.espn.com/classic/biography/s/Hamill_Dorothy.html.

4   People in Sports, "26 Athletes Who Went Completely Broke," Ranker, January 8, 2024, https://www.ranker.com/list/athletes-who-are-broke/people-in-sports.

5   Mike Winters, "The Best- and Worst-Paying College Majors, 5 Years after Graduation," CNBC, March 24, 2024, https://www.cnbc.com/2024/03/24/best-and-worst-paying-college-majors-5-years-after-graduation.html.

6   The 4% rule of thumb is dependent on a variety of assumptions, including asset allocation and inflation among others, and has been challenged over the years as market

assumptions change. It is however the long standing rule of thumb and used for illustrative purposes in this hypothetical scenario.

[7] "History of PBGC," History of PBGC | Pension Benefit Guaranty Corporation, August 30, 2024, https://www.pbgc. gov/about/who-we-are/pg/history-of-pbgc#:~:text=In%20 1875%2C%20the%20American%20Express,also%20 began%20to%20provide%20pensions.

[8] Aaron O'Neill, "United States: Life Expectancy 1860-2020," Statista, August 9, 2024, https://www.statista.com/ statistics/1040079/life-expectancy-united-states-all-time/.

[9] Andrew Dunn, "What Is the Average Home Value Increase per Year?," Intuit Credit Karma, August 30, 2022, https://www.creditkarma.com/home-loans/i/ average-home-value-increase-per-year.

[10] Andrew Dunn, "What Is the Average Home Value Increase per Year?," Intuit Credit Karma, August 30, 2022, https://www.creditkarma.com/home-loans/i/ average-home-value-increase-per-year.

[11] Jing Pan, "Warren Buffett Once Bet $1m That He Could Beat a Group of Fancy Hedge Funds over 10 Years - and He Crushed Them with a Technique Requiring Absolutely No Investing Skill. Here's What He Did," Yahoo! Finance, December 24, 2023, https://finance.yahoo.com/news/ warren-buffett-once-bet-1m-113000485.html?guccounter= 1&guce_referrer=aHR0cHM6Ly93d3cuZ29vZ2xlLmNvb S8&guce_referrer_sig=AQAAAC7AUuQNNs3A9j-2gBi- dq4_KgydKFvHaFUjp_JMVJ96g-a6PDQ_DU4I9xbAfAh CaQtAJrPLKhEOM0aHDYhTELf2KHqO7yPGCdEU0 PSrXesxzSE_GOQG9fa6UGfktKhryeMTYFr1b6zZo9Do DfHlAx7rtZikHmO_S1xkcen2MXmn.

12 "How Many Car Accidents Occur Each Hour, Day & Year?," Amaro Law Firm, March 29, 2023, https://amarolawfirm.com/how-many-car-accidents-occur-each-hour-day-year-in-the-u-s/.

13 "What Are the Chances of Getting into a Car Crash?," Regan Zambri Long Personal Injury Lawyers, PLLC, accessed May 23, 2024, https://rhllaw.com/what-are-the-chances-of-getting-into-a-car-crash/#:~:text=Nationwide%2C%2043%25%20of%20first%2D,involved%20in%20a%20car%20wreck.

14 *Data based off the S&P 500; past performance no guarantee of future results*

About the Author

Joe is currently the owner of New Horizons Wealth Management, a husband, father, and a coach. Helping as many middle-class families as possible is the goal for all his combined ventures, whether it be through advising traditional clients, producing podcasts, authoring books, or producing online resources.

After graduating with honors from The College of New Jersey, he worked for New Horizons Wealth Management for over 15 years, working his way up from intern to financial adviser before eventually purchasing the firm from his mentor and the firm's founder.

His goal for the future is to help over 100,000 middle-class families make their lives more enjoyable by removing financial anxiety and uncertainty through financial education resources.

Joe holds Series 7, 24, and 66 Securities Licenses as well as a CFP® and CFS® designation. He also has Life, Health, and Long-Term Care Insurance licenses.

His wife, Lauren, was a teacher and now works from home as a Lead Social Media Marketer to be able to be there for their children. They reside in the Packanack Lake Community of Wayne, NJ.

In his spare time, Joe enjoys traveling with the family, woodworking, home improvement projects, gardening, and serving as the Grounds Governor for Packanack Lake Community.

CONNECT WITH JOSEPH

Follow him on your favorite social media platforms today.

TheFinancialPinwheel.com

www.ingramcontent.com/pod-product-compliance
Lightning Source LLC
Chambersburg PA
CBHW071420210326
41597CB00020B/3592